Endorsements for *It's OK* ...

"Take a deep breath, relax, and dive into a book that will bring you perspective and peace! Julia Hogan offers a meaningful, faithful, and well-balanced approach to self-care that we all need as beloved children of God. For years, I've longed for a book to recommend to women that discusses self-care within the Catholic worldview. This is that book." — LEAH DARROW, author of *The Other Side of Beauty*

"In an age that often considers self-care to be an extended form of selfishness, Julia Hogan does a great service to her profession, her clients, and her readers by articulating the keys to achieving a balanced and flourishing lifestyle. She approaches her subject in a way that integrates the spiritual, mental, emotional, and physical components of human life. Based in large part on St. John Paul II's understanding of the human person, she provides a practical guide to self-care anchored in timeless insights that lead to true happiness." — FR. CHARLES SIKORSKY, J.D., J.C.L., L.C., president, Divine Mercy University

"Most people cannot understand the difference between self-centeredness and self-care. In a world overrun and confused by narcissism, Julia Hogan has woven together a poignant exposition of the dignity with which we are created in the image of God and the goodness and responsibility we have to show ourselves due reverence in caring for ourselves. We can't give what we don't have, and everyone from healing professionals to ministry leaders to the average man or woman can benefit from her words." — DR. GREG BOTTARO, author of *The Mindful Catholic* and director of the CatholicPsych Institute

"Part fairy-godmother, part psychologist, Julia Hogan reminds us what self-care actually looks like (hint: it doesn't translate to an indulgent trip to the spa). This is more than just a book: it's a guide that will help you uncover what real balance means, helping you tap into your own transformative powers." — MARIA WALLEY, relationships editor at *Verily* magazine

IT'S OK TO START WITH You

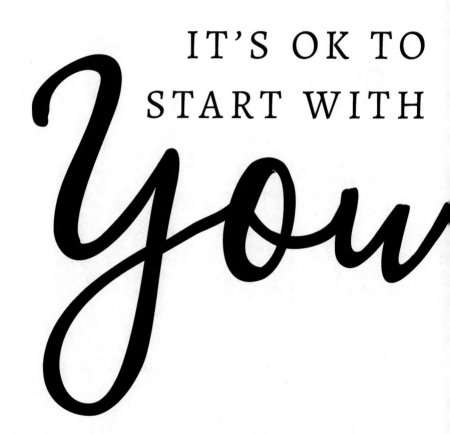

JULIA MARIE HOGAN, MS, LCPC

Our Sunday Visitor

www.osv.com
Our Sunday Visitor Publishing Division
Our Sunday Visitor, Inc.
Huntington, Indiana 46750

Our Sunday Visitor Publishing Division
Our Sunday Visitor, Inc.
200 Noll Plaza
Huntington, IN 46750
1-800-348-2440

ISBN: 978-1-68192-205-8 (Inventory No. T1911)
eISBN: 978-1-68192-206-5
LCCN: 2018935369

Cover and interior design: Lindsey Riesen
Cover art: Shutterstock
Interior art: Shutterstock

PRINTED IN THE UNITED STATES OF AMERICA

About the Author

JULIA MARIE HOGAN is a Licensed Clinical Professional Counselor in Chicago. In addition to her work as a psychotherapist, she leads workshops and writes on topics related to self-care, relationships, and mental health. She is passionate about empowering individuals to be their most authentic selves. You can find more of her writing online at Verily. She completed her Master's in Clinical Psychology at the Institute for the Psychological Sciences in Arlington, Virginia. For more information, please visit juliamariehogan.com.

Dedication

To my parents and my sister, who have always encouraged me to pave my own path, cultivate my talents, and share them with others.

Disclaimer

This book is meant to be for informational purposes only. It is not meant to serve as a substitute for professional medical or psychological help. Please check with a healthcare professional before making any diet, exercise, or other lifestyle changes. If you are in crisis, contact your nearest emergency medical center.

All identifying information in the case examples in this work have been changed. All individuals mentioned in this book are a combination of many clients and do not refer to one particular client, or were created for illustrative purposes.

Table of Contents

Introduction

"I remind myself to be kind to myself, and as slightly ridiculous as it may sound, to treat myself in the same gentle way I'd want to treat a daughter of mine. It really helps."

— Emma Stone, actress

Self-care is a term therapists toss around on a daily basis, but not many people outside the world of therapy have a good sense of what it means. Too often it's mistakenly viewed as an excuse to behave selfishly.

My goal in this book is to challenge that misconception and provide you with the understanding and the tools to create a balanced self-care plan — a plan that will transform your life. Why is self-care so important? Most of us rush through each day running on fumes, fitting in meals where we can or while on the go — if we remember to eat at all — getting little sleep, and feeling perpetually behind. It's not a very fulfilling way to live.

When we aren't our best selves, it shows. Think about it: When you're exhausted and overwhelmed, you simply can't be the friend, family member, significant other, coworker, or boss that you want to be. Even worse, neglecting our well-being makes it nearly impossible to live life as authentic Christians, because we aren't caring for ourselves the way God calls us to. After all, Jesus tells us to "love your neighbor *as yourself*" (Mt 22:39, emphasis added).

It's far too easy to come up with excuses for not taking care of ourselves. We don't have time. Other people (our families, our children, our colleagues, our friends) need us, and we want to be there for them. We put a lot of other things ahead of our own well-being, often because we think we have no choice. After all, this is what being a good person demands of us, right? Of course, we do need to love our neighbor, but we can't do that if we aren't laying the foundation through the habits of self-care. And to lay that foundation properly, we need to be okay with ourselves and with taking care of our physical, emotional, mental, and spiritual health.

Starting with your own well-being gives you the road map you need to become your best self. When you recognize that you're worth taking care of, your priorities shift and become clearer. Nourishing your own well-being frees you to be your best self for others in the specific way that God has called you to, whether that's as a parent, a spouse, a coworker, or a friend.

Authentic self-care is anything but selfish. It's a disciplined way of life that lays the groundwork for everything else, from your work to your relationships. As you read this book, you'll learn tips and tools for prioritizing your well-being in a healthy way, not only for your own good, but so that you can be more fully present and available to others.

How to Use This Book

This book is broken into two parts. Part I makes the case for prioritizing self-care. We are complex creatures, and it's important to understand the reasons why we often fail to take good care of ourselves — and why that's a problem — before we can start making changes to our lifestyle. Part Two breaks self-care down into physical, mental, emotional, relational, and spiritual self-care, explaining why each of these areas should be a priority and offering examples of ways you can put each type of self-care into action. The second section also contains a Self-Care Action Plan and sample plans for your reference.

This book is designed to be an easy reference for you, so approach it in whatever way is most helpful to you right now. You can read the book from cover to cover, or you can flip to the sections that resonate most. Reflection questions or takeaways at the end of each chapter are designed to help you apply the concepts covered to your own life. Separate discussion questions are meant for a group setting and to help spark conversation on these topics. There is also note-taking space provided for you to journal, reflect, and keep notes as you read.

Try to approach this book and topic with an open mind. The ideas and strategies presented here are meant to help you let go of any self-critical thoughts and beliefs that may be holding you back from living a full and authentic life in the unique way God has called you. While I work as a therapist and my job is to help other people heal and live better lives, I am certainly not perfect when it comes to self-care. I know what it's like to encounter self-doubt, and to feel exhausted and overwhelmed. I've been there, and many of the strategies I present here I've used myself and have experienced their benefits. Believe me when I say I know what it's like to try to juggle the demands of everyday life without completely falling apart. But I also know it's possible to find lasting health, peace, and joy. We're in this together!

PART I

Know Your Worth

CHAPTER 1

Why Do I Feel This Way?

"Growth begins when we start to accept our own weakness."
— JEAN VANIER, HUMANITARIAN

What's Really Going On

When Jeffrey came into my office, he appeared to be on a path to success. He was well-spoken, dressed impeccably in a coordinating dress shirt and tie, was well-organized, and projected an air of confidence. He had recently made a career change and had started working for a nonprofit. Fueled by a passion for serving others, Jeffrey threw himself into his work from the moment he started his job. He booked his days full with meetings and projects and stayed up late to answer emails, return phone calls, and plan for the next day. His dedication was admired by his coworkers and bosses.

To the outside observer, Jeffrey seemed to have his life under control. But under the put-together image was another story.

Jeffrey was frustrated by the nagging sense that he wasn't doing enough. His work wasn't bringing him the fulfillment he thought it would. Instead of experiencing a sense of peace in his work, where he was serving people in need, he felt like he could never do enough to meet his own expectations. He relentlessly pushed himself to become even more involved in his work, operating on very little sleep and feeling perpetually exhausted.

"Why do I feel so inadequate if I am doing all of this good work to serve others?" he wondered. If you asked Jeffrey why he threw himself into his work to the point of burnout, he would tell you it was because he saw the great needs in the population he was serving. But deep down, something else was happening.

Over time, Jeffrey came to realize that underneath his hard work and put-together appearance, he didn't really like himself. And it was easier for Jeffrey to ignore this uncomfortable reality by filling his days and nights with work (for a good cause, of course), rather than paying attention to his own needs. He hoped his work could prove to others that he was worth something even if he didn't believe it himself. So he neglected himself and threw himself into his work. At his core, he didn't believe he was worth taking care of.

This belief translated into dangerous habits of neglect. He ignored his own needs because he didn't believe his well-being was a priority. He was not getting enough sleep, not eating properly, not exercising regularly (instead he would exercise intensely in short bursts, then go through long stretches of not exercising), and neglecting friendships and personal relationships. He suffered from depression and anxiety, and, without the protective buffer that self-care provides, his symptoms worsened. Jeffrey's work had become a way for him to bury his deep-seated dislike of himself, and it came at a cost. His mental, emotional, physical, and spiritual health suffered, as well as his relationships.

Like Jeffrey, my friend Anna also didn't believe she was worth taking care of, though she expressed it in a different way. While Jeffrey was driven and motivated, Anna drifted from degree to degree and job to job, never really sure what she wanted to do. She switched her major in college many times and wound up pursuing a master's degree in a field completely unrelated to her undergraduate major. She quickly grew tired of each new job she tried and expressed frustration when it didn't bring her the sense of fulfillment and purpose she was looking for. She would be quick to embrace the latest trend but would also be just as quick to drop it for the next. She never felt confident in herself and her abilities.

Her feeling of being adrift also showed up in her relationships. She often took a very passive role, dating men with strong personalities who dictated the tone of the relationship. There were many times where her friends were concerned that she was compromising her values for the sake of the relationship. Anna, on the other hand, wasn't concerned about the way she was living her life. She found it easier to ignore the feelings of inadequacy she experienced by constantly searching for something new and fulfilling with the hope that the new thing she threw herself into would provide her with the sense of worth she was so desperately seeking.

Both Jeffrey and Anna didn't like themselves very much, though they expressed it in different ways. Neither believed in their own inherent worth, so they neglected to take care of themselves. Jeffrey buried his self-dislike beneath his busy schedule and skimped on sleep, exercise, and proper nutrition, while Anna hid from her low self-esteem by seeking affirmation in unhealthy relationships.

Worth the Effort

Believe it or not, their struggles are not unusual. While not everyone experiences feelings of low self-worth to the degree that Jeffrey and Anna did, many of us are constantly fighting to ignore a nagging voice in our heads that whispers this lie: "*You aren't enough.*"

The busy mom who feels guilty taking time for herself … the overwhelmed college student who believes not earning straight A's isn't an option … the business professional who stays late at work and doesn't make time for relationships … at their core, all share the same struggle: They have a difficult time embracing their own self-worth.

Like Jeffrey and Anna, most of us grapple at some level with the belief that we are unworthy. We deal with it in different ways, often trying to ignore it by burying ourselves in our work, our volunteering efforts, our relationships, etc. We operate under the belief that if we work hard enough and long enough, push ourselves enough, we'll prove to others and ourselves that we are worth something.

Yet this relentless quest to prove our worth is unfulfilling — we never feel enough. All we feel is exhausted, overwhelmed, and inadequate. For many of us, in our fight to prove our worth, we forget to treat ourselves in a way that shows we are worthy of love. Though we are desperately trying to prove to others that we are worth something, the way we treat ourselves betrays what we really think of ourselves. While we might think we're being heroic or virtuous (or we're just too busy), when we neglect basic habits of self-care, the message we're really enforcing for ourselves is, "I'm not worth the effort."

The truth is, you will never be able to "prove" to yourself or to anyone else that you are enough. And that's because you don't have to. Yes, really, it's true. It's paradoxical, but the harder you try to prove you are worth something — whether or not you realize that's what you're doing — the worse you'll feel. Your work, your ministry, even your vocation cannot and will not give you meaning and worth, no matter how much you throw yourself into them. Why? Because the simple fact is, you are looking in all the wrong places. You are enough. The very fact that you exist means that you are worthy of love.

To dig ourselves out of the lie that we have to prove our worth, we need to start living like we believe we are worthy. That means learning to live by the discipline (because, yes, it's a real discipline) of self-care. It's okay to love yourself. In fact, you should!

And before you object, saying, "I'll sleep when I'm dead," or "Taking care of yourself is self-indulgent and a waste of time," hear me out: As Christians we believe that God has a purpose for us. He calls us to something greater and more meaningful. He calls us to be stewards not only of the other people he's put in our lives, but also of ourselves — of the body, mind, and talents he's given us, that make us who we are. And that's where self-care comes in. Only when we take care of ourselves can we offer our best selves when we go out into the world to serve others in whatever way God has called us to.

Self-care is anything but self-indulgent. In fact, it can be hard work to take care of ourselves. It's hard to go to bed on time when you're binge-watching your favorite TV series, and even harder to drag yourself to the gym when you'd rather sleep in. But it's worth the effort. *You* are worth the effort.

Taking better care of yourself starts with baby steps, simple adjustments in your daily patterns of acting, speaking, and even thinking. It won't happen overnight, but as you begin to build these habits, over time I can promise you will experience the sense of peace and fulfillment you've been missing from your life.

Remember, you are worth it!

....

Reflection Questions

1. Do you recognize any similarities between Jeffrey's overworking and his struggle to invest in his well-being, or Anna's constant search for the next new and exciting experience, and your own struggles?

2. In what ways do you find it most challenging to take care of yourself physically, mentally, emotionally, spiritually?

Discussion Questions

1. Why do you think failing to take adequate care of our own physical, emotional, mental, and spiritual needs is so common in today's world?

2. Why do you think it's sometimes easier to serve others than to attend to our own needs?

CHAPTER 2

Being Mean to Ourselves

"People, even more than things, have to be restored, renewed, revived, reclaimed, and redeemed; never throw out anyone."

— AUDREY HEPBURN, ACTRESS

The Voice in Your Head

Kristina was a client of mine who struggled with low self-esteem. She would tell me how she hated her appearance: "I'm so fat and ugly." She tried diet after diet, starting strong for the first few days but then giving up, telling herself she could never expect to succeed. And her indulging in self-pity would often end with a trip to the gas-station convenience store to pick up her favorite junk food. Her reasoning was, "I'll never lose weight anyway, so I may as well eat what I want." She was stuck in a cycle of feeling defeated and overwhelmed by self-pity. All the while, her inner critic told her that, unless she lost the "perfect" amount of weight, she was a failure in life. Since she didn't believe she could actually follow through with her diet, she felt trapped by her self-dislike.

Like Kristina, we all have an inner critic. What does the voice inside your head tell you? Typically, your inner voice is your harshest critic and zeros in on your deepest, darkest insecurities. It's easy to recognize your inner critic because it tends to deal in absolutes and worst-case scenarios. For example, your inner critic might tell you that you'll bomb your presentation at work because you have no idea what you're talking about (even though you spent hours preparing for it). Or maybe it whispers that because your kids have been extra crabby lately, you are the worst mother ever (even though you've had plenty of proud and meaningful parenting moments). Perhaps your inner critic insists that no one will ever want to be in a relationship with you because you aren't attractive, smart, or funny enough (even though you have a track record of positive relationships in the past).

Your inner critic's specialty is ignoring positive qualities and zeroing in on flaws, magnifying them so that they seem more real and terrible than they actually are. This relentless and constantly running monologue is an unwelcome reminder of your insecurities, flaws, and doubts. Whatever your inner critic tells you, it always leaves you feeling terrible about yourself and, at its worst, defeated and hopeless.

When we listen to our inner critic, we start to believe that the lies it tells us over and over are true, and then we start to act as if they are true. It's a fact of our human nature that when we hear something repeated over and over again, we start to believe it's true (even if it's not). What happens when we listen to the repeated lies of our inner critic? Often, we start to neglect our well-being on some level, either because we believe the inner critic when it tells us we're not worth it, or because we're trying so hard to prove it wrong that we don't give ourselves permission to invest in our well-being. These habits of neglect might start to show up in little ways such as not getting enough sleep, indulging in escapes like TV or junk food, letting our exercise routine fall by the wayside, or allowing ourselves to feel inferior to everyone else whether comparing looks or talents. And, if left unchecked, this self-neglect can snowball and become much worse over time, creating or exacerbating many other problems.

Trying to Prove the Voice Wrong

Though Kristina's experience was an extreme example of the way negative self-talk holds us back, many of us allow similar self-defeating thoughts to sabotage our lives and make us miserable. Listening to the inner critic fuels the underlying belief that we aren't good enough just as we are, and that we are unworthy. This perpetuates the cycle of not feeling good enough: I don't like myself very much, and my inner critic reminds me constantly that I'm not perfect, so this, in turn, reinforces my belief that I'm not good enough. It's a painful cycle to be in, and a tough cycle to break.

Different people tend to deal with this critical inner voice in different ways. Some of us get stuck in the same old bad habits of self-sabotage. Like Kristina, we respond to our belief that we are damaged or flawed by setting ourselves up to fail. Procrastination is an example of this that most of us can relate to. (Sometimes I think I'm an expert procrastinator when it comes to writing!)

If you're a procrastinator, think about the last time you were facing a deadline and ask yourself why you put off working on that project. Perhaps deep down you were afraid you didn't possess the qualities needed to perform well. By waiting until the last minute to complete a project, you have a built-in excuse if the project doesn't turn out the way you hope. "I ran out of time," or "I could have done a better job if I wasn't rushed," is a lot easier to deal with than, "Even though I had plenty of time, I struggled with this project and I still didn't do as well as I'd hoped, and now I feel like a failure." Fearing that you don't have what it takes can be intimidating, so, often, it's easier to give yourself an excuse than to face even the possibility that you aren't perfect. The trouble is, none of us is perfect, and mistakes will happen — but making a mistake doesn't mean you are a failure. If you make unrealistic perfection your standard, you will always be disappointed.

Others respond to the inner critic by throwing themselves into work or other projects, pushing themselves to the breaking point in an effort to prove the negative thoughts wrong. The often-unspoken motivation is: The more power I have, the more important I am; the bigger the number on my paycheck, the more I can prove to my inner critic that I really am worth something.

I personally experienced this during my graduate training in Washington, D.C. While I made several meaningful friendships and professional relationships, there seemed to be a general attitude in the city that power, busyness, and self-importance were more important than meaningful connections and relationships. Often, people were more interested in the networking and opportunities a new acquaintance could provide someone than in an authentic relationship. There was an uncomfortable undercurrent of "I'm only interested in what you can do to help me further my career" in many social interactions. At social events, the first question asked was, "What do you do?" Far from being a harmless question, this turned potential new friendships into transactions, like we were in a game of one-upping each other. I distinctly remember someone telling me with pride that they "worked on the Hill." I knew very well that they were interning for the summer and probably just fetching coffee and making copies, but they wanted to make themselves sound as important as possible.

Others fight their inner critic by spending all their energy trying to ensure that they are well-liked and that everyone is happy with them. I'm reminded of an old acquaintance of mine who used to try to buy the friendship of others. He would insist on unnecessarily covering the check at birthday dinners or buying expensive gifts for friends and acquaintances alike. Often, people would try to take advantage of his generosity. In reality, he didn't have much confidence in his likability and tried to mask it by excessive generosity.

Unfortunately, when we measure our self-worth by a paycheck, or by the power we have, or by how much people like and admire us, sooner or later it backfires. The truth is, we're never satisfied when it comes to power, money, or the admiration of others, and we will always want more. Yet power, money, and the admiration of others can disappear in an instant. They're not a reliable foundation on which to base your self-worth.

How to Recognize and Reject That Inner Voice

Often, we don't even realize that there's a running monologue of self-defeating thoughts in our heads until we take a step back to look for them. Usually, we just accept these thoughts as fact and let them guide our actions. And the more we listen to and accept these thoughts as facts, the more deeply ingrained they become.

But I will let you in on a little-known fact: Just because you have a thought doesn't mean that thought is true. Really! Think about how many times you've had a random thought appear out of the blue. For example, maybe your friend has been acting evasive lately when you try to make plans for dinner with them. You can't help but think maybe they don't want to spend time with you anymore. But is this true? Maybe. But it could also be that your friend is being evasive because they are planning a surprise birthday party for you, or they are distracted by a stressful work week or a difficult family relationship. Once you know the facts, it's easy to see that your initial belief wasn't actually accurate.

Our thoughts are not always true, but some thoughts are easier than others to dismiss. Most of our thoughts aren't very powerful — or, as I like to say, very "sticky" — but the thoughts our inner critic feeds us are *very* sticky for some reason. Yet the thoughts your inner critic feeds you are simply … not … true.

Take a step back and ask yourself what that voice inside your head is telling you. What kind of lies is it feeding you on a daily basis? If you've never tried to stop the lies your inner critic is feeding you, it can be difficult even to recognize them at first, because they are so deeply ingrained. Here's a clue to help determine whether your negative thoughts are coming from your inner critic or from your authentic (and more accurate) self: if the thought is negative and coming from a place from fear, it's probably your inner critic.

For example, many of my friends and I can have trouble accepting compliments. Even something as simple as "I love your scarf" can be uncomfortable to hear. It's easier to respond with, "Oh, I couldn't decide what to wear this morning so I grabbed this in a hurry, but it's actually a pain to wear," when a simple "Thank you!" would have been sufficient.

Why is it so hard to accept a compliment? For many of us, it's because we believe it when our inner critic tells us we don't deserve it. A "congratulations" or a "job well-done" on a work project, or even a compliment on our physical appearance, seems like a lie. Rather than boosting confidence, compliments serve as an uncomfortable reminder that we aren't happy with ourselves.

Similarly, we all have those friends who are always apologizing, even if something isn't their fault. Their emails, texts, and phone calls always begin with "Sorry to bother you, but … " While it seems harmless enough, this simple phrase communicates that they feel like they are imposing on us and our time, as if they have to preemptively apologize for asking a simple question. Here's a tip I've found helpful in conquering this habit: Whenever I find myself starting an email with an apology, I delete the apology and dive right into the reason why I am emailing.

That pesky inner critic can also show up when we talk negatively about ourselves to other people. Phrases like, "I'm so lazy," "I'm not good at XYZ," and "I'm sorry I'm so boring," are all ways our critical inner voice leaks out. It's our way of expressing that we aren't happy with ourselves.

The inner critic constantly reinforces any false belief we may have that we are unlovable, unworthy, and never enough.

Like Kristina, we can let this voice keep us from lifting ourselves up and striving for our goals. It tells us that we'll never amount to anything, and we ask ourselves why we even try. If we can't do it perfectly, we may as well not do it at all, we tell ourselves. At the same time, we hold ourselves to impossible standards of perfection that we don't expect from anyone else. It's understandable if other people make mistakes, but we think *we* should never make mistakes, because that indicates we are stupid and weak. Other people may struggle to keep their lives together, but *we* have to maintain perfect work/life balance or we're failing in our relationships. We love many other people who may not be beautiful or successful by any worldly standard, but unless *we* lose a certain amount of weight, look a certain way, have a particular job, make a certain amount of money, or own a particular type of home, we are failures. The trouble with holding ourselves to standards of perfection is that we will always be disappointed because (news flash!) no one is perfect.

Sometimes it's easier to see this when it comes to other people. We are quick to offer words of support and encouragement when someone else is struggling in any way. Why do we withhold that same kindness from ourselves?

While we may not neglect ourselves to the same extent as Kristina (or Jeffrey and Anna from the previous chapter), our belief that we aren't worth taking care of can show up in many other ways. When day-to-day life seems overwhelming, zoning out in front of the TV eating a bowl of cereal is much easier than dragging ourselves to the gym for a workout. Skimping on sleep is somehow easier than getting to bed on time. We'd rather stay up late watching TV, which inevitably means getting up in a rush the next morning, after hitting the snooze button one too many times. Neglecting self-care can also look like snacking on a candy bar instead of eating a well-balanced meal, or feeling like you have to say yes to every request at work or favor asked by a friend.

When we listen to our inner critic, we give in to not expending the time and energy it takes to take care of our needs. And we can be very creative with our excuses for neglecting self-care. Typical excuses include:

- I don't have the time.
- I don't have the energy.
- People need me (family, coworkers, friends).
- That time in front of the TV is the only "me time" I get in a day.
- What are you talking about? I'm fine — I don't need much anyway.

Do any of these sound familiar? If you consistently relegate your own well-being to the back burner, you probably need to take a look at what's going on. Why are you so bent on achieving impressive things in your work, to the detriment of your health? Why do you bend over backward to make sure everyone likes you? Or why do you keep falling back into the bad habits and cycles that leave you feeling miserable and defeated? On some level, you're probably listening to that mean voice in your head — or trying your hardest to prove it wrong.

Silence Your Inner Critic

Listening to our inner critic and neglecting self-care are often deeply ingrained and, because of this, it can take time to learn a new way of thinking about ourselves and our self-worth. For most of us, that inner voice is a melding of many factors that have joined forces over the course of our lives to become the self-critical monologue we hear in our heads on a daily basis. Negative childhood experiences, criticism from our parents or other adults in our life when we were children, difficulty in school, friendship struggles, relationship challenges, and body-image issues all contribute to the formation of the inner critic. While everyone's negative voice sounds different, unfortunately, no one is immune.

Thankfully, you don't have to let your inner critic sabotage your life. You can break the cycle of self-defeating thoughts and actions.

Stopping the cycle begins with silencing that inner voice. It's time to make a change. When you ignore your own needs, you set yourself up for long-term misery, and over time you reinforce the lie that you're not worth the effort. It starts with small habits of neglect, such as regularly skimping on sleep, or consistently trading healthy meals for more convenient but less healthy takeout. Over time these small habits can snowball into bigger ones, like letting relationships slide. The result? You're stressed, overwhelmed, overtired and exhausted, overworked, under-confident, and lonely.

To silence your inner voice, start by challenging it. Refuse to accept what your inner critic says as gospel truth. Even if the inner voice tells you it's not worth it, take practical steps to care for your emotional, physical, and spiritual well-being. In the beginning it may feel counterproductive because your inner critic's voice is so loud, but that's okay. Keep challenging it.

That critical voice might tell you there's no point in working out because it won't make a difference. Challenging that voice means working out anyway and giving yourself the opportunity to experience the benefits of exercise. That critical voice might tell you that you have to say yes to every request that comes your way. Forget the fact that your calendar is completely booked, if your friend asks for your help planning a surprise party, you feel the pressure to say yes. Challenging your inner critic means acknowledging your schedule is overbooked and sending your regrets to your friend. The more you challenge the lies your inner critic feeds you, the quieter that voice will get, the better you'll feel (emotionally and physically), and the more you'll believe that you are lovable and worthy just as you are.

Be Kind to Yourself

Taking better care of your physical, emotional, mental, and spiritual

well-being means changing the way you treat yourself each day —
beginning with the way you speak to (and about) yourself. Commit
today to being as kind to yourself as you would be to anyone else.
Try to be kind when thinking about yourself. Try to be kind when
speaking to yourself. Try to be kind when you are feeling run-down
and lousy. Try to be kind when you are struggling with a tough
situation. Treat yourself with kindness.

Hang in there and don't give up. Not only is treating yourself
with kindness important and beneficial for you, it's a road map to
becoming the most authentic version of yourself. And the wonderful
thing about living a full and authentic life is that it has a spillover effect.
You are a better friend, parent, daughter, son, coworker, partner, etc.,
to the people in your life. When you radiate the knowledge that you
are a unique human being worthy of being loved, it's contagious, and
others experience it and benefit from it.

Reflection Questions

1. What specific lies does your inner critic tell you?
2. Are there particular times/situations when your inner critic's
   voice becomes louder?
3. How does believing your inner critic negatively affect your life?
   How do you neglect your self-care as a result of the inner critic's
   lies?

Discussion Questions

1. What kind of impact does a person's inner critic have on their
   emotional, physical, and spiritual well-being?
2. Why do we so easily accept the lies our inner critic tells us about
   ourselves, yet immediately see the lies when our friends speak
   badly of themselves? Why do we hold ourselves to a different
   standard?
3. Think of the people you know who radiate healthy confidence.
   What makes them different from those people who aren't
   confident?

CHAPTER 3

Stressed-Out

"When the well's dry, we know the worth of water."

— Benjamin Franklin, American statesman

Busy, Busy, Busy

Neglecting basic habits of self-care, like getting adequate sleep and nutrition, makes us vulnerable to stress and its potentially damaging effects, which can trap us in a cycle that's difficult to break out of.

It doesn't help that today's society celebrates being busy. We equate having a packed schedule and getting little sleep with being important. A common reply to the greeting "How are you?" is, "Busy; so busy." (I've definitely caught myself saying this more than a few times.) While it may be true that your calendar is booked, being "so busy" really means: "I am so busy because I am important and my time and talents are in demand. You should be appropriately impressed." Society tells us the busier you are, the more important you must be.

In an opinion piece for *The New York Times*, "The 'Busy' Trap," Tim Kreider observed: "Busyness serves as a kind of existential reassurance, a hedge against emptiness; obviously your life cannot possibly be silly or trivial or meaningless if you are so busy, completely booked, in demand every hour of the day."

Many of us overbook our schedules in order to feel important, worthy, and needed, but it comes at a cost. We may *feel* important, but we also feel stressed, overwhelmed, sleepy, drained, irritable, even sad. Is being negatively affected physically and emotionally because of our busyness really worth it? Do we value feeling important and needed more than our physical and emotional health?

Being busy in the quest to be important perpetuates a cycle of negativity that is difficult to get out of and increases our risk for stress. Stress is such a common occurrence that the American Psychological Association (APA) conducts a survey on the effects of stress on Americans every year. In the 2014 APA survey, 42 percent of adults said they did not believe they were doing enough to manage the effects of stress in their lives. The study also found that the most common effects of stress included feeling irritable or angry, feeling nervous or anxious, having a lack of interest or motivation, fatigue, feeling overwhelmed, and being depressed or sad. So, if several of the symptoms described above have a starring role in your life, you're not alone. Stress is a nationwide issue.

The effects of stress include:
- trouble falling asleep or staying asleep
- muscle tension
- digestive issues
- weak immune system
- difficulty concentrating during the day
- increased irritability
- headaches
- forgetfulness
- social isolation

The Slippery Slope
The effects of stress, whether related to work, relationships, or health, have a way of sneaking up on us. For example, if it's the busy season at the office and you're feeling stressed and overwhelmed, you might start to have trouble falling asleep at night because your mind

is racing, thinking about everything you have to do tomorrow, and your body is keyed up and tense from being on the run all day. You just can't relax. And if you are going to bed later than normal and having trouble falling asleep, you aren't getting quality sleep. When you aren't getting enough sleep, you won't be as alert the next day. The effects are compounded over time, and those occasional sleepless nights become the norm until, eventually, you're chronically sleep deprived. It's a slippery slope.

When left unchecked, stress can become burnout (chronic stress). Typical symptoms of burnout include consistently experiencing exhaustion, difficulty concentrating, irritability, difficulty sleeping, low motivation, lack of interest in activities that you previously enjoyed and found meaning in, and feeling like you are in a mental fog. Living with burnout is like running on fumes when your gas tank is empty, and it can be difficult to recover from. That's why it's critical to manage the effects of stress in its early stages so that you aren't faced with a long-term recovery from burnout.

Let's say you've been under stress lately, and you are starting to notice some of the effects of stress in your life. What does this mean? It is often a sign that you aren't making yourself and your health a priority. That's when you have to ask yourself the probing question: Why aren't you treating yourself like a priority? True, it can be an uncomfortable question to ask, but it's crucial.

Too often we settle for living in misery without reflecting on what's causing it and without challenging it. A busy student assumes that skimping on sleep is a normal part of being in school and lets her schoolwork take precedence over her health. A young professional tells himself that he's too busy to cook and regularly orders greasy takeout, prioritizing his work over his health. A new parent begins to believe that day-to-day life with a newborn is meant to be perpetually overwhelming, exhausting, and isolating. When we live our lives by these beliefs, we chip away at the buffer that protects us from everyday stress, making us more and more susceptible to its effects.

To make matters worse, exhaustion, difficulty concentrating, headaches, and other effects of stress make us more likely to react badly to the curveballs life throws us. Work deadlines, car trouble, or relationship struggles become more difficult to deal with, leaving us feeling drained and rundown. We lose our resilience and our ability to bounce back when we're battling the crippling effects of stress.

It's important to listen to what your body tells you so you can recognize the effects of stress. These signs are often the first clue that you aren't taking care of yourself adequately. Being able to recognize these symptoms in their early stages allows you to make the necessary changes to take care of yourself and prevent the effects of stress from taking over your life. (Stay tuned, we'll cover how to do this step by step in Part II of this book.)

Blurred Boundaries

Not taking care of ourselves also impacts our relationships and the way we interact with the world around us. If we already struggle to believe in our own worth, we're more likely to allow other people to determine our worth, which sets us up to be used and taken advantage of by others. Boundaries become blurred and we end up spending more and more time fulfilling the requests and needs of others instead of meeting our own needs. This is backward, because taking care of our own needs actually enables us to maintain healthier relationships, while not taking care of ourselves has the opposite effect. When we don't take care of ourselves, we aren't able to be fully present to others or be our best selves in our relationships.

Blurred boundaries typically happen in one of two ways: (1) either we let ourselves become overwhelmed by the demands others place on us because we struggle to set boundaries and to say no, or (2) we let our schedules become over-packed because we like to feel that we're needed and important.

In the first case, we end up with a lot of resentment. I had a friend who worked for a nonprofit organization whose mission he felt very passionate about. He enthusiastically embraced any project he was given and was first to volunteer to work the company's special events on weekends. Over time, however, he started to feel tired, overwhelmed, and emotionally drained by the job he loved. Why? The leadership took advantage of his dedication and asked for more and more of his time and energy, until he felt as if the company owned his schedule. He was asked to work long hours and to lead difficult phone calls and meetings on behalf of the leadership. Yet his dedication was never acknowledged by those at the top. My friend grew resentful of the leadership and ultimately left the organization with a bad taste in his mouth. Like my friend, we can grow resentful toward others when we neglect to prioritize our self-care and set boundaries.

In the second case, which is often subtler, the sense that we are doing something good for others can become a sort of substitute for authentic self-love. We thrive on the rush that comes from feeling needed and wanted by others, and we help and serve others to make ourselves feel wanted, loved, and needed. A former colleague of mine lived this way. She was always willing to help others with their projects. If a coworker was facing an impending deadline, she would stay late with them at the office to help, even at the expense of getting her own work done. She lived for their praise and expressions of eternal gratitude once the project was completed. While this might seem like a noble and unselfish act, the truth was she needed to be needed. She didn't feel worthy just as she was, so she sought out the validation of others to have a sense that she was worthy.

We need to recognize and believe in our inherent worth outside of the good we do for others. If we help others only because we need validation and affirmation, are we really helping in an authentic way? Our motive should never be because helping others helps us feel good about ourselves. Instead, we want to be able to see our neighbors' needs and meet them, regardless of how (or even if) they thank us.

The Buffer Effect

How does all of this relate to self-care? When you take care of yourself by eating well, exercising, getting quality sleep, investing in healthy relationships, and being mindful of your emotional, mental, and spiritual health, you build a buffer that protects you against the negative effects of stress. Life happens, but if you can stick to certain basic habits of self-care, you'll be much better prepared to deal with anything life might throw your way.

You don't have to live with the negative effects of stress on your life and in your relationships. You're worth more than that. While we can't ever get rid of all the things that cause us stress, we can take positive action to ensure stress doesn't have the final say in our lives. By making simple, small changes in your everyday life (which will be laid out in detail in Part II), you can break the cycle of stress and begin to build a new and more authentic way of living.

....

Reflection Questions

1. What are the symptoms of stress you most commonly experience?
2. Do you measure your worth by how busy you are? What could you cut from your schedule to get back just a little more time to take care of yourself?

Discussion Questions

1. Why do you think our culture equates being busy with being important? What can we do to push back on that idea?
2. What are some steps we can take to maintain (or repair) clear boundaries in our relationships?
3. What are good guidelines for us to know whether or not we are helping others with pure intentions?

CHAPTER 4

What Is Self-Care?

"We are not the sum of our weaknesses and failures;
we are the sum of the Father's love for us and our real
capacity to become the image of his Son."
— POPE SAINT JOHN PAUL II

L iving like you're worth it will mean building a whole new set of habits. Silencing your inner critic is an important part of the process, but it's not the whole story. The full answer lies in learning how to practice authentic kindness — to yourself.

If this concept makes you uncomfortable, then you probably have a wrong understanding of what self-care really is. Given the way it's talked about in pop culture and society at large, it's understandable if you approach self-care with some skepticism. Self-care is "in" now, and the label gets slapped on many things that are not truly helpful or good for us. Even worse, it can be used as an excuse for selfish behaviors and attitudes that are unkind and damaging to ourselves and others. This is not what authentic self-care is.

True self-care is much more than a collection of sayings or self-indulgent, surface-level practices. It's a way of life that reinforces the fact, rooted in our dignity as God's children, that we are worth love and care. It's a set of habits, built over time, that takes seriously the Gospel command to "love your neighbor *as yourself*" (Mk 12:31, emphasis added).

You Are a Gift

The kind of self-care we're talking about involves treating yourself and those around you with the compassion and kindness that comes from the deeply rooted conviction that you are worthy of love. Authentic self-care is living your day-to-day life in a way that recognizes you are seeking to be the most alive version of yourself. And self-care is lived out in the little ways on a daily basis by choosing to get enough sleep, exercising, eating properly, and fostering healthy relationships. It involves daily practice, and it can be slow going at times. It takes perseverance. It's not a quick fix.

There's nothing selfish about this. As Christians, we believe that God calls us to love and serve others. In other words, we are called to be a gift to others. Think about this practically. When you give someone a gift, you select it carefully, thinking about that person, their likes and dislikes. If it's homemade, you create the gift with that person in mind. You wrap the gift carefully in fun wrapping paper or a nice gift bag. You would never grab a half-eaten box of chocolates and throw it into a grocery bag to pass off as a gift for your friend's birthday. (I'll bet some of you even shuddered at the thought when you read that. I know I did.) The same applies to each of us in our call to be a gift to the people in our lives. Not only are we called to be a gift to others in our own unique way, but we are called to be the best gift that we can be.

That's where self-care comes in. If you don't take care of yourself, then you can't be a very good gift for others. When you are stressed, exhausted, and having a hard time liking yourself, you can't be an intentional gift to others.

It can also be helpful to think of yourself as an instrument for God's purposes, like a paintbrush. When you are unkind to yourself, all you have to offer him is a worn, tired, sparse paintbrush. But when you take care of yourself, you are a shiny, sleek, full paintbrush that can be used to create great works of art. Taking care of yourself (physically, emotionally, spiritually, relationally) is the way to be the best instrument for God and his grace, not only in your own life, but in the lives of others.

Keep in mind, too, that receiving gifts graciously is just as important as giving gifts thoughtfully. (Remember when your mother always made you say "thank you" when you received birthday gifts and all those thank-you notes you had to write after Christmas?) When you believe that you are worth it, you are able to receive gifts from others without feelings of guilt or embarrassment. You can accept with gratitude that this person wants you to know how special you are to them. When you know your own worth, you are able to express gratitude when others affirm you.

High Standards

We can let ourselves be ruled by the belief that we have to be perfect and that we can never make mistakes because attaining perfection is the only way others and God will truly love us. We set impossibly high standards for ourselves, and those standards aren't based in the reality of who we are. The truth is, no one is perfect, so when you make a mistake (and you will, because you're human!) you can't hold that against yourself. But your inner critic is really good at telling you that you have to be perfect all the time, no matter what, or else no one will love you. When you believe this, you withhold mercy and forgiveness from yourself, and you shut yourself off from receiving love.

I recently went on a retreat where the priest talked about the importance of letting our mistakes go. He explained that while we can't become immune to our sins and mistakes, we also can't let them weigh us down. God finds you lovable, just as you are right now, even with your imperfections. There is nothing you can do to make God love you less. That message hit me like a ton of bricks. I had never heard God's mercy and compassion explained that way.

Let me repeat that: There's nothing you can do to make God love you less.

In fact, when we try to be "perfect" all the time, we hold ourselves to a standard that God isn't calling us to. (The perfection God wants from us is all about love. It has nothing to do with never making mistakes. It has to do with always striving to grow closer to him and become more like him.) God forgives our sins and forgets them; we should try to cultivate that same healthy detachment from our sins, imperfections, and mistakes. Acknowledge them, make a plan to move forward, and move on. Don't carry them around like dead weight. Ask yourself: Does withholding compassion from yourself help you grow and live the vocation God has for you? God wants to give us forgiveness, compassion, and mercy, if only we're brave enough to ask for it. That's a pretty big deal!

While we tell ourselves that we aren't lovable because we haven't met an unattainable standard of perfection, God, in his infinite wisdom, is loving us authentically and unwaveringly through it all. If you were the only soul on earth, God would still send his only Son to come into the world to save you. You are that important to him.

I worked with a client who made a mistake early in her career that shaped her professional trajectory in a way she never anticipated or wanted. She turned down a job offer because she felt intimidated by the people she would be working with and didn't believe she would be successful at the job. But almost immediately after she turned the offer down, she regretted her decision because it would have been an opportunity for growth. Yes, it would have been challenging, but it would have also helped her develop valuable skills that would have propelled her career forward. For years, she would relive her early mistake thinking: "If only I hadn't done that. I should have known better. Now nothing will ever be the same. How will I ever recover?" She tortured herself with the thought of how things might have been if she hadn't made that mistake. Her fixation on her mistake and her disappointment in herself kept her stuck in the past instead of looking forward.

Whether it's in a career, a relationship, or some other aspect of our lives, all of us may allow ourselves to get stuck on our past mistakes. We let them become defining moments of our lives, in a negative way. We think of ourselves as "the person who made a terrible mistake and should have known better" instead of "the person who is learning as they go, who sometimes makes mistakes, and who knows they aren't perfect." Don't let your past mistakes keep you from believing in your inherent worth. Remember God's love for you and try to live your life with that knowledge as your guiding beacon.

Give Yourself Permission to Live in God's Love

Try this exercise: Think of a time when you had an authentic experience of God's love. It could be when you were going through a really rough time and a friend came to your rescue; a powerful experience while enjoying nature; a moment in church; or any situation where you were made aware of God's presence in a powerful way. These moments give us a tangible sense of God's love, which helps us trust in that love even when we don't really feel it in our day-to-day lives. If you have never had this experience, I encourage you to ask God for it — I promise, he wants to give it in the way that's perfectly suited to you, your personality, and your needs. And keep an eye out — often we aren't even aware of his presence because it can be subtle, in a whisper instead of a lightning bolt.

Our imperfections and failures can actually bring us closer to God. He can use our mistakes and sins to guide us to become the best version of ourselves and to live in relationship with him. But we have to let him. The first step is practicing forgiveness and compassion to ourselves when we make mistakes. God does not want you to stay stuck in the past, chained to your sins and mistakes. He asks you to accept his mercy and forgiveness, to treat yourself with compassion, and to move forward with hope and confidence that you'll do better in the future.

While treating yourself with kindness and compassion might seem like abstract concepts, luckily, there are concrete ways that you can live out these ideals. This is what authentic self-care looks like. This is where the rubber meets the road and where abstract theory meets the practical. This is where the why meets the how. When you make your physical, mental, and spiritual life a priority, you are showing yourself and others that you believe in your own self-worth. Even more importantly, you give God's love room to become a tangible reality in your daily life. It is then you give God permission to love you in the way you treat yourself, because you are removing the self-doubt, self-dislike, and other negativity that stands between you and God.

Remember, practicing compassion and kindness toward yourself isn't about being perfect, it's about taking care of yourself in the best way you can, wherever you are in life. You are not called to a false standard of perfection, but to be the most authentic version of yourself — so you can be a gift to God and to others. Let go of the false belief that you have to be perfect; instead aim for doing the best you can, knowing that that is enough. You are enough.

....

Reflection Questions

1. Does the idea of self-care make you uncomfortable? If yes, why?
2. Think of a moment when you have received true kindness and love from someone else. How did that person treat you? Now think of a moment when you gave true kindness and love to someone who needed it. How can you allow these experiences to inform the way you treat yourself, especially when you're going through a difficult time?
3. Are there mistakes, failures, or sins from your past that you have trouble letting go of? What's one past mistake you can hand over to God's mercy and forgiveness?

Discussion Questions

1. After reading this chapter, has your understanding of self-care changed? If so, how?
2. Why do you think we have trouble letting go of the need to be "perfect"? Does our culture perpetuate this false belief?
3. How could practicing self-care open you up a little more to receive the love of God?

CHAPTER 5

What Self-Care *Isn't*

"If a little flower could speak, it seems to me that it would tell us quite simply all that God has done for it, without hiding any of its gifts. It would not, under the pretext of humility, say that it was not pretty, or that it had not a sweet scent, that the sun had withered its petals, or the storm bruised its stem, if it knew that such were not the case."

— Saint Thérèse of Lisieux

When I tell people I'm a therapist, they assume that I have my self-care routine down pat. Sometimes, I think my clients see me as a Mary Poppins: "practically perfect in every way." But that just isn't the case. Remember when you were younger and you assumed your teachers lived at school, and how exciting and mystifying it was to see them in the "outside world"? I remember seeing a teacher grocery shopping, and I was absolutely fascinated. But, of course, teachers have their own lives outside of the classroom. It's the same with therapists! We have lives outside of our work, and that life comes with everyday stresses and challenges. So, I know what it's like to struggle to find enough time for sleep, to set boundaries in relationships, and to silence my inner critic. I am walking right alongside you in this journey toward embracing our inherent worth and the practice of self-care.

The term self-care wasn't even part of my vocabulary until I began graduate school. Prior to that, I had the attitude that I had to make everything work out, no matter what. What if I needed to dog sit, finish my thesis, put in time at my internship, go to class, and plan an upcoming birthday party for a friend all in one day? No problem, I'd tell myself. And, yes, I was able to do it all, but at the expense of my own well-being. I was exhausted all the time, and all I wanted to do was sleep; for a few months I was perpetually sick. It was awful, but I kept pushing forward to make it all work, because that was the unspoken expectation I had set for myself.

When I learned about self-care and how crucial it is to our overall well-being, it was a game changer. Just knowing how important self-care was to managing stress and minimizing its effects gave me the motivation to make taking care of myself a priority. Once I knew that getting enough sleep would give me more energy, help me focus better at work, and boost my memory, I started taking my sleep routine seriously. Once I acknowledged that I couldn't say yes to every invitation or professional opportunity that came my way, it was freeing to politely decline so that I would have more time to focus on the things I had already said yes to. While I'm still learning how to take the best care of myself, I can personally attest to the difference making yourself a priority can make in your life.

However, while self-care is a common topic of conversation in the world of therapy and mental health, it isn't that common anywhere else, except maybe in women's lifestyle magazines. Practicing self-care is a little-known secret, but it shouldn't be because of its amazing benefits. Just by picking up this book and starting the hard work of making your well-being a priority, you are way ahead of the game. Take a moment to acknowledge and appreciate the hard work you've done so far (seriously, do it!).

Misconceptions about Self-care

Unfortunately, many people have an incomplete understanding of what authentic self-care truly is, which leads to a lot of criticism, especially in Christian circles. It's likely you've come across many of the common misconceptions, whether in written articles or in conversation with your friends. Some critique self-care as a short-term "band aid" technique, more a mindless form of escapism than an authentic method of taking care of yourself. Others say it's ineffective. Still others view it as purely selfish, trying to turn self-indulgence into a health necessity.

Let's address and correct misconceptions about self-care. Remember, authentic self-care is being kind to yourself and is one of the best ways to embrace your dignity and self-worth. When we don't take care of ourselves, it becomes much harder to live the authentic life we've been called to live. The stress and difficulties of everyday life can become overwhelming; our physical, emotional, and spiritual health suffers; and it becomes more difficult to believe that we're really worthwhile. We're always operating from a place of frustration with our lives and ourselves, and the cycle goes on and on.

Following is a look at the most common misconceptions about self-care, in light of everything we've said so far about living like you're worth it.

Misconception 1: Self-care is a temporary and ineffective "fix."
Many argue that stress-relief strategies such as listening to calming music, watching a funny video, or calling a friend don't get to the root of stress, low self-esteem, relationship challenges, or other problems. Instead, these practices just help us feel better in the moment, without solving the real problems. This argument misses the point of what authentic self-care really looks like, both in theory and in practice.

Strategies like these are only a small part of the whole practice of self-care and are not meant to serve as complete or permanent solutions to stress, feelings of worthlessness, or feeling unlovable. Self-care strategies alone can't cure deeply rooted feelings of unworthiness, but when integrated into a larger plan and a new way of looking at yourself and at reality, they can be powerful tools to help you truly believe that you are worth it.

It's true that simply engaging in select self-care strategies recommended by therapists won't leave you feeling fulfilled. But, as discussed in Chapter 4, making these practices a regular part of your routine can reinforce over time the new patterns you're trying to establish internally: silencing your inner critic and allowing yourself to believe that you are worth it. These are truly long-lasting, life-changing practices.

Misconception 2: Self-care is selfish and un-Christian.
One of the most common misunderstandings is thinking that taking care of yourself is selfish. Shouldn't we be spending our time serving others? Won't acts of service and love make us feel better more effectively than getting enough sleep and eating our vegetables? Isn't it selfish to say "no" when others request our help? In other words, doesn't self-care make us turn inward, focusing on only our needs and ignoring the needs of others? Isn't that un-Christian?

If that was all there was to self-care, then, absolutely, we would need to avoid it as Christians. But true self-care is not self-indulgent. It's about practicing a healthy, very Christian, love for ourselves so that we can love others effectively and fully.

A popular saying is, "You can't pour from an empty cup." When you are completely empty, you have nothing to give to others, but when you keep your cup full, you can share with others in much more meaningful ways without draining yourself. Taking care of your own well-being is like keeping your cup full. Practicing self-care allows you to be really present to others, and it keeps you from running dry.

True self-care is anything but self-indulgent pampering. In fact, it takes a lot of discipline — something that's definitely in line with Christian principles. For example, getting up early to exercise is anything but self-indulgent (especially in the winter). Why would we commit to it? Because regular exercise improves our physical and mental health. To look at another example, it takes a lot of willpower to say "no" when a friend asks for your help. We don't like people being angry with us, after all! And, of course, sometimes (in emergencies, for instance), we need to set ourselves aside to help another person in need, but often we have to look honestly at our own limitations and graciously decline if we don't have the time, or if the other person is taking advantage of our generosity.

Authentic self-care isn't turning inward and forgetting the needs of others. Rather, it is acknowledging (and deeply believing in) your dignity and worth. It is treating yourself with the care that you deserve. It's holding yourself accountable to your need to take care of yourself, knowing that, if you want to really be present to others and serve them in an authentic way, you have to be secure in your own well-being. From this perspective and understanding, taking care of yourself isn't a selfish undertaking, but rather an important part of authentically living out your calling in life — whatever that may be.

Misconception 3: Self-care is for the weak.
Some people view self-care as a cop-out, only for those who aren't tough enough to push through and soldier on. Self-care is for the weak, and in this world only the strong survive.

Let's take a step back and reconsider these ideas. The truth is, life isn't a competition to see who can get by on the least amount of sleep or food, or with the most caffeine. Pressing pause to make sure you are taking care of your physical, emotional, and spiritual needs is not a sign of weakness. Actually, it takes a lot of discipline. It's not always easy, and it certainly is not a sign of weakness. On the contrary, it's a sign of strength and humility to acknowledge that you can't thrive on sheer willpower day in and day out.

Misconception 4: Self-care is a waste of time.
Let's face it, most of us are pretty sure there are a lot of other, more important, ways we should be spending our time. Why waste precious hours on sleeping, exercising, eating, praying, and most of all playing when we should be making a difference in the world?

Think about it this way: How can you change the world when you're exhausted, stressed, or burnt-out? All you can give others in that case is the distracted, depleted version of yourself. Setting aside time to take care of yourself may feel like taking time from other things you should be doing, but it's time well spent. Too often we have a skewed view of what time well spent actually means. When your priorities are making more money, making others happy, and being constantly busy, taking the time to take care of yourself looks like a complete waste of time. But, when your priorities are taking care of your physical, mental, and spiritual well-being, knowing that this builds the foundation for a healthy and flourishing life, self-care is unquestionably time well spent.

To go back to the pouring-from-an-empty-cup analogy, when you set aside the time to take care of yourself, you are replenishing your cup so you can go back out and serve others. Running from activity to activity at the expense of your health eventually leaves you with nothing left to pour. It's most definitely not the best use of your time.

Misconception 5: Self-care is about being perfect.
Some people mistakenly think that taking care of yourself means being on a quest for perfection. Before they even start, they are overwhelmed and discouraged.

As we discussed in Chapter 4, though, self-care is not about being perfect, it's about taking the necessary steps to be the best and most authentic version of yourself — imperfections and all. In fact, believing in your worth means accepting imperfections and working within your own particular limits. Striving for complete perfection will always leave you feeling disappointed. On the other hand, seeking to better yourself will help you move forward with confidence.

Excuses, Excuses

Now that we've debunked the most common myths about self-care, it's time to look at the other major obstacle: our own excuses. These can be deep-seated, and it's important to bring them to light, examine them, and start moving past them if we want to live life to the fullest.

"I don't know how."
Not sure how to practice self-care and embrace the most authentic version of yourself? Don't worry, I'll walk you through exactly how to do this in the second half of this book. I'll cover several different categories of self-care, suggest easy-to-implement strategies, and provide you with a blueprint as you begin your journey. Don't feel overwhelmed. I'll show you how and where to start. Just keep reading!

"I don't have the time."
Yes, we all lead busy lives, and adding another item to your endless to-do list probably doesn't sound appealing. But practicing kindness to yourself doesn't have to take up very much time. Especially as

you're starting out, working self-care into your life means making small changes over time. The most lasting and effective changes are the ones made slowly and deliberately. It's all about taking small steps and reminding yourself that you are worth the effort.

Ultimately, it's worth the time you devote to it. Practicing self-care is not just another relaxation strategy or lifestyle fad; it's a shift in mindset that will allow you to better manage your time. It will free you to say "no" to the things that hold you back from being your authentic self and allow you to say "yes" to the things that help you embrace the person you were created to be.

"*I'm not worth it.*"

If you are still wrestling with self-doubt, remember that being kind to yourself, even in small ways, helps you live as if you believe in your self-worth. Actions can help influence beliefs, so acting like you already believe you are worth it can help you better understand that you are, in fact, worth it. In other words: fake it till you make it.

"*I'll become self-centered.*"

Scared that taking care of yourself will make you selfish? While it's true that focusing too much on yourself *is* selfish, that kind of lifestyle is not authentic self-care.

Remember that practicing self-care is a means to an end, not an end in itself. It's you acknowledging your inherent dignity, even when you don't feel it, and it allows you to embrace your authentic self. What's more, you can only really serve others when you are your best self. By making self-care part of your life, you're keeping yourself healthy and fit so you can love others in a truly generous way. That's not selfish at all!

"*I'll just be taking the easy way out instead of working hard.*"

Scared of giving in to weakness? Don't forget that you can't be really strong unless you're healthy: physically, mentally, emotionally, spiritually. Self-care isn't always easy. Going for a run when you'd rather stay under the warm covers isn't easy. Saying "no" to a pushy friend who might get upset at you isn't easy. Having the courage to practice kindness to yourself is definitely not taking the easy way out.

Don't let these or any other excuses hold you back from being kind to yourself. You deserve the opportunity to experience the life-changing benefits of self-care, and combating excuses is critical.

Don't be afraid to say "yes" to self-care! If you don't start with you, you won't be able to love or serve others, either.

....

Reflection Questions
1. What self-care misconceptions have you come in contact with?
2. Which excuses do you find yourself using when thinking about taking better care of yourself?
3. Are there any fears that you have about starting to take better care of yourself? How can you combat these fears?

Discussion Questions
1. Why do you think many people are resistant to embracing self-care and its benefits?
2. Why do you think many people find it intimidating to start practicing self-care?

PART II

*Creating Your
Self-Care Plan*

CHAPTER 6

Getting Started

"Love yourself first and everything else falls in line.
You really have to love yourself to get anything done
in this world."

— LUCILLE BALL, ACTRESS

I n the first half of this book, we covered why it's so difficult to focus on taking care of ourselves and what the antidote is to the faulty belief that we're not good enough. We dove into the big ideas behind why it's okay to start with ourselves when it comes to seeking authenticity and fulfillment in life. But now it's time to transition from the *why* to the *how* of self-care. This is the exciting part where you'll gather ideas to help you better invest in your well-being.

Remember, you are worth taking care of. But, sometimes, whether it's the stress of life getting you down or listening to the constant lies of your inner critic, that can be hard to believe. How do you make yourself believe it? It's actually pretty simple: you have to live it. And to live it, you have to practice kindness toward yourself.

As you start to think about how you can incorporate self-care practices into your daily life, it can be helpful to take a step back and look for patterns in your life. Let's start with the positive. Where in your life are you really thriving when it comes to self-care? Are there any good habits you've built up on a regular (or even semi-regular) basis? Take some time to list those areas and celebrate what you're already doing. Even something as simple as getting enough sleep most nights of the week, eating vegetables every day, or taking the stairs instead of the elevator at work is worth noticing and celebrating. When you do these things, make it a point to tell yourself: *I'm doing this because I believe I'm worth it.* This practice will help reinforce the message and set you up to build more good habits going forward.

Now let's take a look at the areas where you want to grow. Ask yourself: Where are my pain points? What areas of my life could benefit from an extra focus on self-care? Make a list (or a mental note) of the top two or three areas where you would like to improve over the next few months.

Before we start building a self-care plan, I've assembled a quick self-care assessment to help you identify where you are doing well when it comes to self-care and where you could benefit from focusing more. This questionnaire will also help you determine how best to use this book going forward. Not every chapter that follows will be necessary for you right now. It is my hope that you'll pick the areas that are most applicable in your life today, and as time goes on you can move on from those chapters and try others, according to your needs.

While it might be tempting to try to make all the changes you want at once, I encourage you to take it slow and focus on one change at a time. You know that feeling after a particularly fruitful retreat or motivating workshop when you're inspired and energized? You leave with all these amazing ideas for ways you are going to improve your life and you can't wait to start. But then, after a few days, the reality of everyday life sets in and you start to feel discouraged. Perhaps getting up at 5:00 a.m. for exercise, prayer, and learning Italian was biting off more than you could chew. And then you start to feel overwhelmed and defeated, and your new goals quickly disappear into thin air.

We don't want that to happen with your self-care plan! While it's certainly important that you feel excited about the changes you want to make, it's equally important that you be smart about your strategy for implementing these changes. Making small changes over time is the most sustainable way to make a lasting change in your life. Keep this in mind as you read the second half of this book. Keep track of all of the changes you want to make, but don't try to make them all at once. Pick one change — for example, adding thirty minutes of Pilates to your day for exercise — and focus on weaving that into your life. Once you have a good handle on that change, consider adding another. It takes patience (sometimes a great deal of it), but it's the smarter way to make effective, lasting changes.

Once you complete the questionnaire you can jump to the chapters that focus on the areas you have identified as needing improvement. As you complete the questionnaire, don't be afraid to be honest. Choose the answer that best describes what you are *currently* doing and not what you *wish* you were doing. This isn't a pass/fail assessment. Rather, it's a starting point for living the authentic life you've been dreaming of.

Self-Care Assessment

Circle the answer that best describes your actions right now. At the end of the assessment, there will be scoring instructions and helpful feedback on your score.

Sleep

I get less than seven to eight hours of sleep a night.	Agree / Disagree
I have trouble falling asleep easily.	Agree / Disagree
I generally watch TV or scroll through my phone before falling asleep.	Agree / Disagree
I wake up frequently at night.	Agree / Disagree
I wake up feeling tired.	Agree / Disagree

Nutrition

I frequently skip meals (especially breakfast).	Agree / Disagree
I find myself mindlessly snacking when bored and/or going to the fridge and pantry when I am stressed.	Agree / Disagree
It is hard to find the time to cook well-balanced meals on a regular basis.	Agree / Disagree
I turn to frozen meals or takeout more than once a week.	Agree / Disagree
I rely on caffeine to combat tiredness or exhaustion on a regular basis.	Agree / Disagree
A cup of strong coffee is the first thing I need before I can start the day.	Agree / Disagree

Exercise

I rarely exercise three to four times per week.	Agree / Disagree
I intend to exercise but make excuses and eventually talk myself out of it.	Agree / Disagree
I avoid exercising because the thought of going to the gym seems overwhelming.	Agree / Disagree
I rationalize not exercising because I tell myself I'll never be able to get fit anyway.	Agree / Disagree

Body Image/Perception

When I look in the mirror, my first thought is a litany of all of the things I don't like about my body and appearance.	Agree / Disagree
I find myself neglecting my appearance because I don't like the way I look.	Agree / Disagree
I find myself comparing how I look to others whether it's identifying ways I don't measure up to the other person's appearance or identify ways I look better than they do.	Agree / Disagree
I tend to place great emphasis on having the right clothes, makeup, and accessories so that people like my appearance.	Agree / Disagree
I am constantly trying a new diet or exercise program with the hopes that it will finally help me achieve my "ideal" body.	Agree / Disagree
I think negatively about my appearance, often multiple times a day.	Agree / Disagree

Mood/Emotions

I find myself worried, stressed, and overwhelmed most days.	Agree / Disagree
I sometimes feel like my emotions are out of control (crying easily, feeling on edge and irritable all the time, or feeling on the verge of an angry outburst).	Agree / Disagree
I tend to ignore my emotions because I'm uncomfortable with what I'm feeling.	Agree / Disagree

Self-Talk/Confidence/Self-Esteem

I think I have low self-esteem.	Agree / Disagree
I often find myself feeling less confident than others in my social circles.	Agree / Disagree
I often think negative thoughts about myself and my abilities — for example, "I'll never be able to do this" or "I'm not good enough."	Agree / Disagree
I don't believe my friends really like me, but that they are just being nice to me.	Agree / Disagree

Social Media

When I scroll through my social media newsfeed, it triggers negative feelings toward myself, jealousy, envy, or frustration.	Agree / Disagree
I find myself avoiding social media because of the above.	Agree / Disagree
I spend a lot of time on social media. Even though I don't find it fulfilling or restorative, I find myself doing it anyway.	Agree / Disagree

Stress

I experience stress on a daily basis.	Agree / Disagree
I experience some or all of the following when I experience stress: muscle tension, difficulty concentrating, digestive issues, a weakened immune system, trouble falling asleep and staying asleep, increased irritability, more frequent headaches, forgetfulness, or a tendency to isolate myself from family and friends.	Agree / Disagree

Leisure

I think leisure activities are a waste of time.	Agree / Disagree
I feel like there is no time for hobbies and relaxing during the day because I am so busy.	Agree / Disagree
I would like to schedule time to relax but find that my other obligations take priority.	Agree / Disagree

Relationships and Boundaries

I feel like I give more than I receive in my relationships.	Agree / Disagree
I find that people frequently count on me to pick up the slack and maybe even assume that I will.	Agree / Disagree
I find it hard to say no when others ask favors of me even if I don't have the time or energy.	Agree / Disagree
I feel like people take advantage of me and my kindness.	Agree / Disagree
I would describe myself as a people pleaser.	Agree / Disagree
I am afraid of upsetting others and place their happiness over mine.	Agree / Disagree

Work/Life Balance

I feel unfulfilled by the work I do.	Agree / Disagree
Work is a source of great stress for me.	Agree / Disagree
I feel unappreciated by my boss and coworkers.	Agree / Disagree
My work life takes precedence over my personal life — for example, I find myself skipping activities in my personal life because I am working late or on the weekends.	Agree / Disagree

Prayer Life/Spiritual Life

I would like to incorporate prayer into my daily life but find it hard to do so.	Agree / Disagree
My spiritual life often takes the back seat.	Agree / Disagree
I wonder why God would love me, and I believe that I am unworthy of his love.	Agree / Disagree

....

Now, look back through your answers. Most likely, in some areas you've circled "Disagree" for most. That's great! That means you're doing pretty well taking care of yourself in those areas.

This questionnaire is meant to help you narrow your focus to those areas of your life where you could benefit the most from a self-care plan. In sections where you answered "Agree" to most (or all) of the statements, you could probably benefit from taking time to invest in your self-worth by developing self-care practices in those areas. For example, say you answered "Agree" to all of the items under the sleep section. This could mean that focusing on your sleep habits would be a good place to start.

We'll take a closer look at how to construct and implement a self-care plan for each of these categories in the chapters to come. For now, just take some time to identify and reflect on the areas where you could benefit from being more intentional about your self-care.

Be proud of yourself for coming this far! It isn't easy to acknowledge that you aren't getting as much sleep as you should or that you could be better about making exercise a regular activity. But remember, no one is perfect, so don't think of these as reasons to beat yourself up. You need to know where to focus to make your self-care plan a success, and you have taken the important step of identifying the areas where you can benefit most from self-care. You're mapping out the best path to achieving your goals. You've begun the exciting and rewarding adventure of becoming a better version of yourself. The assessment you just took is essential to making these exciting changes a reality.

CHAPTER 7

Taking Care of Your Body

"Our bodies are our gardens to which
our wills are gardeners."

— WILLIAM SHAKESPEARE, PLAYWRIGHT

Most of us have a love/hate relationship with our bodies. Trust me, I've experienced this. When I have an impossible to-do list, sleep and proper meals are often the first things to go. I know I will function better if I take care of my body and brain, but it can be difficult to accept my limitations. I wish I was someone who could thrive on four hours of sleep, but I'm not. And I know that if I want to be at my best, sometimes I have to hit pause on my to-do list and take care of myself.

Neglecting our physical well-being has a ripple effect on our whole life, not just physically, but mentally, emotionally, and even spiritually. It can be helpful to look at physical self-care as an investment in your health, a chance to take care of the body that makes it possible for you to do great things. Without your body, you can't be the parent, spouse, friend, or professional you want to be, nor can you do the work that you are called to. Being kind to your body is in your best interest — and it's not impossible, I promise.

I ask you to keep an open mind as you read through this chapter.

You don't have to throw your career and lifestyle away so you can sleep ten hours a night; I won't be urging you to start training for a marathon or to become a bodybuilder; you don't have to embrace some extreme diet. I'm just asking you to take an honest look at the current state of your physical health. You might find that there are small changes to your routine that will make a world of difference in your quality of life. Give yourself the chance to experience the benefits of taking care of your physical health.

You are the only person who can take control of your physical health. No one else can do it for you. You have to believe in the power of investing in your physical health, and you have to be the one to start making changes. Remember, change is best sustained when made in small increments. While it is completely okay to have many goals for improving your physical health, don't try to implement them all at once. You'll soon feel overwhelmed and discouraged. Instead, pick one change to make and really focus on that one before adding another.

The four main areas of physical health that we're going to focus on are sleep, nutrition, exercise, and body image. All of the recommendations I make are supported by research, but I encourage you to talk with your physician about any questions or concerns you have before you make any changes. I also recommend finding a trusted nutritionist and personal trainer to help make sure you are taking care of your body in the way it needs.

Sleep

Are you constantly running on fumes? If your motto is "I'll sleep when I'm dead," it might be time to take a step back and honestly evaluate how that motto is working for you. Did you know that when you are sleep deprived there is less activity in the frontal and parietal lobes of your brain — both of which are important for decision-making and problem-solving activities? While you might feel like you are accomplishing more when you get less sleep, the quality of your work and mental functioning actually suffers.

If I asked you what you think about the amount of sleep you are currently getting, what would you say? (Go ahead, think about it!) My guess is you would tell me you wish you got more sleep, but that you don't know how it's possible.

Sleep is not a "nice to have" luxury that few can afford. It's a necessity for your physical, mental, and spiritual health. I've learned that prioritizing sleep is key to being at the top of my game during my workday. If I've had a late night and know that I need to get quality sleep so I'll be prepared for the next day, I will skip my workout for that day. I always struggle with this decision, because my inner critic pipes up and tells me that skipping one day will derail all of the hard work I've put in, but I know that it's ultimately the best decision.

Sleep is essential to your emotional and physical well-being, and research confirms it. Research has found that getting enough quality sleep is linked to a better immune system, weight management, lowered risk for diabetes and heart disease, improved mood, reduced stress, and increased ability to concentrate during the day.[1]

On the other hand, not getting enough sleep has been linked to an increased risk of high blood pressure, brain fog, obesity, and difficulty concentrating.[2] It has also been found to contribute to difficulty making decisions and solving problems, and to increased difficulty managing your mood.[3]

I get it. Life is busy, and it can be hard to wind down at the end of the day. If you're like me, your mind swirls with thoughts about the day that's coming to a close, with tomorrow's plans, and with your worries, fears, and concerns. I call it the hamster wheel: just when we should be drifting off to sleep, our brains suddenly jump into action, spinning with a million different thoughts.

When I'm working with my psychotherapy clients, sleep is one of the first things we focus on when creating a self-care plan. Very rarely do I have a client who is getting the Centers for Disease Control and Prevention's (CDC) recommended seven to eight hours of sleep a night. In fact, their sleep routine is often nonexistent. Remember when you were a child and you had a bedtime routine? Around a certain time each night you had a snack, brushed your teeth, put on your pajamas, read a book or two, sang a song, and got tucked in. This routine helped you wind down and signaled to your brain that it was time to start getting ready for sleep. While our routine might look a little different as adults, we can still benefit from a sleep routine.

What does your effective sleep routine look like? To start, identify how many hours of sleep you need and what time you need to get up on a typical day. For example, let's say you need seven and a half hours of sleep and you need to get up at 6:30 a.m. That means you need to be asleep by 11:00 p.m. Here it's important to note that you need to be *fast* asleep by 11:00 to get the full seven and a half hours. Sliding under your covers at 11:00 isn't going to get you the sleep you need, unless you are one of the lucky ones who can fall asleep as soon as your head hits the pillow. Allow yourself twenty to thirty minutes to fall asleep. Watching the clock and calculating the fewer and fewer hours you have until you have to get up in the morning when you're having trouble falling asleep is a stressful experience, so give yourself ample time to fall asleep to help remove that pressure. This means that if you need to be asleep by 11:00, you'll want to be in bed by 10:30.

Once you've established your bedtime, it's time to create a routine for yourself. It doesn't have to be elaborate and overly complicated. The ingredients of a successful sleep routine involve calming activities to help power down your brain and body. And consistency is key. Ideas include a warm bath, listening to soothing music, using lavender essential oils, journaling, reading, praying or meditating, and light stretching. Pick one or two activities that you enjoy and that are doable. It's also important to avoid screen time (the blue light signals to your brain that it should stay awake) and bright lights. It's a good idea to make your room as dark as possible to help you fall asleep faster. That means watching TV right before going to bed isn't a good idea. (Cutting out TV before bed may not be a popular strategy, but it is a very helpful one.)

It can be helpful to keep your phone in another room when you're going to sleep. Your smartphone is a wonderful tool, but it is also an incredible source of distraction because it provides easy access to social media, news updates, videos, and games. Powering your phone down before bed helps to eliminate these distractions. If you typically use your phone as an alarm clock, consider purchasing an inexpensive digital clock to use instead.

A sample routine might look like washing your face and brushing your teeth at 10:00 p.m., followed by a hot bath and ten minutes of prayer and journaling before getting into bed and reading for a few minutes before you start to feel drowsy. Plus, you'll be right on time to start falling asleep around 10:30 so that you'll be deep asleep before your official 11:00 bedtime.

A simple bedtime routine is all it takes. Not only is it good for you, it actually feels good, too — and it's not that hard to implement. It will require only a few small adjustments.

Action Plan

1. Establish the time you need to be asleep each night so you will get seven to eight hours of sleep. Remember to give yourself twenty to thirty minutes to fall asleep.

---

2. Take a moment to envision your ideal bedtime routine. What would it look like? Go ahead and jot down the activities that sound most relaxing and appealing to you right now and map out a rough schedule. The key here is to create a routine that is easy to implement even on the busiest days when your motivation is lowest. For example, if you've had a nonstop day, will you actually light a candle, take a hot bath, journal, and stretch before going to bed? Probably not. It might be better to commit to journaling for ten minutes and do five minutes of stretching before climbing into bed. A fifteen-minute bedtime routine is very doable, while a thirty- or forty-minute routine won't always be possible. Stick with a plan that you can do every night, no matter what.

Fuel Your Body and Mind

What you eat plays an important role in your physical and mental health. When you live a busy life, food can often be an afterthought. Running late for work? Maybe you'll grab a banana or a granola bar as you rush out the door (I've definitely done this before). Or perhaps you just skip breakfast altogether. I personally know several people who skip breakfast or lunch without a thought. Or they grab fast-food or whatever is easily available — and, unfortunately, the convenience of fast-food usually means sacrificing nutrition.

Taking the time to prepare and eat nutritious meals can seem like a hassle, but there's a clear link between what we put in our bodies and our mood. Research shows that the majority of the neurotransmitter serotonin — which helps regulate appetite, sleep, and mood — is produced in the gastrointestinal tract.[4] What you eat influences the production of this neurotransmitter. There's also plenty of research that indicates that diets rich in vegetables, fruits, unprocessed grains, fish, and seafood, and limited amounts of red meat and dairy are associated with a lower risk of depression.[5]

I've personally experienced how what I eat influences how I feel. After a stressful time in graduate school, I was constantly tired even though I was getting plenty of quality sleep. When I brought it up to my doctor, he recommended that I try eating more protein. I took his advice and noticed a significant difference in my energy levels. I had been concerned that something more major was going on from a health perspective, when really it was just that I wasn't eating enough of the right foods.

If you're still not convinced that seeking out healthful foods is worth the effort, try to think of food as delicious fuel for your body. Keep in mind, too, that there isn't a one-size-fits-all approach when it comes to food. Try to figure out what kinds of foods give you the energy and nutrition you need. When in doubt, find a nutritionist you can trust. I've figured out that I do well on lots of protein, so I make sure that is part of every meal, even if I have to make a quick protein shake. I have friends who thrive more on carbohydrates and others who need more vegetables. It may take some time to get to know how your body responds to different foods, but once you find the right combination, it will make a positive difference in how you feel about yourself.

Comfort Food

For some, food can become a coping strategy for stress or any negative emotion. Others find they always eat when they are bored. If you've experienced this, very likely you often don't realize you are using food to deal with unwanted feelings. The key here is to recognize when your impulse to raid the pantry is a response to a negative feeling. It's important to be intentional about your reasons for eating. Before you open that bag of chips, ask yourself: "How am I feeling? Am I hungry — or am I eating for some other reason?" Then be honest about how you're feeling and anything that might have happened over the course of the day to trigger those feelings.

The important thing is to make a conscious decision rather than letting your emotions dictate when (and what) you eat. If you are trying to escape a negative emotion, take a few seconds to acknowledge that you are feeling badly, try to figure out why you are feeling that way, and then try to problem solve. Is there some kind of action you can take besides eating that can help you feel better? If so, take it! If not, take some other positive action. Rather than eating a snack, call a friend or go for a walk.

For example, one of my clients who was working on taking better care of herself told me that she found herself reaching for her candy drawer at work whenever she was stressed. Using a recent experience as an example, together we worked backward from the time she opened the candy drawer to figure out what had triggered this response. We figured out that a meeting with her boss that morning during which she received some critical feedback had left her feeling stressed, overwhelmed, and self-critical. Just making this connection between the stressful event and her impulse to eat something that tastes good was an eye-opener for her. When she knew the reason behind her impulse to overindulge with sweets, she was able to take steps to address the root problem: her self-critical thoughts.

It's also important to remember that healthy eating doesn't necessarily mean dieting. I've had many clients who tell me that they signed up for a weight-loss program only to abandon that diet within a few weeks. When it comes to self-care, healthy eating means committing to a sustainable way of life, one you can stick with over the long-term.

It's not about "good" versus "bad" foods, it's about making food choices that fuel your body while giving yourself permission to enjoy the delicious foods that are out there. One healthy rule of thumb here is the "80/20 rule": 80 percent of the time you eat healthy foods, and 20 percent of the time you allow yourself some leeway. For example, say you are traveling and are at a business dinner. Normally, you wouldn't order dessert, but since it's a celebratory dinner for a project well-done, you have dessert without berating yourself for choosing to enjoy it.

Yes, a "quick fix" can be appealing, which is why crash diets sometimes seem like a great option, but these intense, restricted diets simply are not sustainable. What's worse, the cycle of dieting and quitting and dieting again fuels our inner critic. Every time we put food in our mouths, it becomes a judgment: "I just ate a brownie, so I blew my diet — again. No surprise, I always blow my diet." Or, "I have no self-control, so why do I even bother trying to eat healthy foods?" Instead, the ideal is to enjoy eating. Food is a gift that fuels your body and supplies some healthy enjoyment.

Remember that the most effective and sustainable changes are not part of a crash diet but are made slowly over time. Don't think you have to completely overhaul your diet today. Instead, pick one small way you are going to take a step toward fueling your body with the nutrition it needs. Maybe that means committing to eating breakfast daily instead of skipping it, or perhaps ordering the vegetable side instead of the cheese fries when you go out to eat. It could also mean choosing to have dessert only one or two times per week, instead of every night. The possibilities are endless, and you just need to figure out what works best for you.

Action Plan

1. It's time to be honest. Identify some areas where you tend to make unhealthy eating choices.

_____

_____

_____

_____

2. List three to five ways you could take a step toward incorporating
    healthier habits into your diet. Now, pick the one you'd like to start
    with this week. After two weeks of consistently implementing
    this habit, consider adding another healthy habit.

_____

_____

_____

_____

_____

The Power of Exercise

I think most of us have a love/hate relationship with exercise, no
matter how often we do it (or don't). We know we _should_ exercise
because it's good for us, but we're also very good at coming up with
excuses not to. Often, we'll start a great workout routine, only to
have it fade after a few weeks or months, and then we're back to
little or no exercise each day. But exercise is a great, tangible way to
practice taking care of yourself. It's not always easy, but it's worth the
investment.

Exercise has been linked to both long-term and short-term
benefits when it comes to mood and overall well-being. For example,
you can expect to experience a boost in your mood after about five
minutes of working out at a moderate level.[6] Regular exercise can
also help reduce the symptoms of depression in the long-term, and it
can help us better manage the symptoms of anxiety.[7] Other benefits
include improved sleep quality, stress relief, increased energy,

weight loss, increased alertness, reduced cholesterol, and increased cardiovascular fitness.[8] Because of these powerful benefits, it makes sense that exercise should be an important part of your plan to take better care of yourself.

If you find yourself resistant to the idea of exercise, it might be useful to consider what your expectations and assumptions are when you think of it. For example, maybe exercise to you means running on a treadmill, bored out of your mind. Or perhaps exercise is linked to years of fruitless chasing after the "perfect" body. These types of thoughts can become barriers to making exercise a regular part of your life.

Exercise isn't just running on a treadmill. It can be any type of movement. I have friends who hate running but love spin class. Some people I know spend most of their time weight lifting, others cross-train. It's all about finding the type of exercise that resonates with you. Try to think of exercise as more than a weight-loss strategy or a way to achieve a perfect body. Instead, think of it as a long-term investment that boosts your overall health, physical and mental.

Adding exercise to your day not only takes care of your body, it also gives you a constructive sense of accomplishment. Yes, it can be hard to actually get yourself to the gym, but once you're there, you're always glad you went. While I may have to work really hard to motivate myself to go for a run in the morning, I never regret it when I get home. And I often remind myself of it when I'm getting ready to start my run. I tell myself that once I start running, I'll be glad I did — and I always am.

The CDC recommends about thirty minutes of moderate activity five days a week, but, remember, it doesn't have to be done all at once. Consider breaking up your workouts into smaller chunks — that is, ten minutes — to make it more manageable.[9] You could take a quick, moderately intense, ten-minute walk in the morning, at lunch, and after dinner. You could even ask a friend to join you so you get exercise and socializing in at the same time. That sounds easy, right?

Exercise can take many forms. It's all about finding what works best for you.

Action Plan

1. What kind of physical activity do you enjoy doing? Jot down three to five activities that you could see yourself easily engaging in at least on a weekly basis.

2. What time(s) of day is (are) best for you to exercise?

3. What are some barriers to exercise for you? What are some practical steps you can take to remove those barriers? (For example, "Joining a gym is too expensive, so I'll use YouTube exercise videos instead." Or, "It's easy to talk myself out of working out in the morning, so I'll pack my gym bag the night before and lay out my workout clothes.")

4. What kind of exercise plan would you like to have? Map out a rough exercise plan that you can fit into a typical week.

_____

_____

_____

_____

_____

_____

Battling Negative Body Image

Your perception of how your body looks is also an important part of taking care of your physical well-being. Due to social media, advertisements, magazines, movies, and TV shows, we're bombarded with images of what the "ideal" person looks like. And while we know objectively that these images are usually Photoshopped and altered, we still allow them to dictate how we feel about our own bodies. We beat ourselves up for not having the perfect body and tell ourselves that someday we will diet and exercise until we are able to meet that perfect standard.

The trouble with comparing yourself to an unrealistic standard is that you are beating yourself up over something that isn't real — meaning it's an impossible goal. If what you see in the magazines is your standard for what you should look like, then you will always be disappointed. Instead of aiming for "perfection," aim for appreciating the body you have been given and the amazing things it can do. Your legs allow you to travel where you need to go, your arms help you carry those heavy groceries (or kids!), and your face communicates your thoughts and feelings to those who are important to you in life.

Letting go of the pressure to achieve the perfect body can be a freeing experience. Instead of beating yourself up for not looking a certain way, you can begin to appreciate the body you've been given. I remember having a very simple yet transformative experience in my beliefs about body image when I was in graduate school. I liked to run along the Potomac River after classes because it helped me to decompress after a long day of listening to lectures and taking notes. One hot and humid day, I ran past a young mother who was jogging and pushing her child in a stroller. I could tell just by the way she ran and her appearance that she was a dedicated runner, but she had a very average body type. She didn't have a traditional thin runner's physique, but she looked strong and healthy. As I ran past her, I had this realization that being fit and strong did not necessarily mean being thin, and that completely changed the way I thought about what it means to be healthy and fit. It was such a simple, everyday experience, but it was a tangible example of what having a positive body image looks like.

Instead of focusing on what you would change, focus on what you like about your body. I encourage clients who struggle with body image to stand in front of the mirror and identify at least one thing they like about themselves. Then, over time, I encourage them to identify more and more qualities they like about themselves. You can try this technique if you consistently find yourself zeroing in on what you dislike when you see your reflection in the mirror.

It's also important to take care of your appearance. Your outside appearance, for better or worse, is the first impression people have of you. When you take care of your appearance, it sends the message to others that you know your inherent worth and that you deserve respect. Often, when people don't feel good about themselves, the way they dress communicates that to others, whether it is oversized clothing, worn fabrics, or unflattering cuts.

Your outward appearance shows others how much you value your internal qualities (and hopefully that's a lot). It isn't shallow or vain to invest some time and energy into your appearance. There is a reason that makeover reality TV shows are so popular. We love seeing people experience the amazing boost of confidence that comes from a haircut that flatters their facial features, clothes that fit and flatter, and makeup (for the ladies) that emphasizes their best features. When we feel good about how we look, we feel more confident about ourselves.

Looking good doesn't mean you have to have a designer wardrobe. It simply means putting in the necessary time and effort to groom and dress in a way that communicates your worth. This means wearing clothes that flatter your body type (this goes for men and women alike) and taking time to style your hair, wash your face, apply makeup, etc. This helps you start your day on the right foot, and it's a way of reinforcing the message — for yourself and anyone else you meet — "I matter and want to treat myself in a way that proves that to myself and to anyone I interact with today."

Take an honest assessment of how you take care of your appearance right now. It might be hard to acknowledge that you neglect some aspects of your appearance, but it's an important (and brave) step to take. Then identify some easy ways you can improve. This might mean investing in a few wardrobe items that fit well without hiding you and that you feel good wearing. You may even find these items at thrift stores — it's not a matter of spending a ton of money, but of looking for quality and fit. I have many friends who have developed a knack for finding flattering clothes at thrift stores. They are some of the best-dressed people I know, so they are living proof that dressing well does not have to break the bank.

For women, other ways to jump-start taking care of your appearance could include visiting the makeup counter at your local beauty store and getting some recommendations from a makeup artist about how to enhance your best features. Or finding a hair salon where the stylists can give you a quality cut and good recommendations for daily care. For men it could mean giving yourself an extra ten minutes to shave each morning, or focusing on other aspects of grooming such as keeping your nails well trimmed and ensuring your clothes are clean and pressed.

Remember the gift analogy? If you are called to be a gift to others, you want to give a well-loved and well-cared-for gift, not one that you dislike. This means loving the body God gave you to do good in the world. Be intentionally thankful for the body you have!

Action Plan

1. Do you struggle with negative body image? How do you allow the "ideal" body to negatively affect your sense of self-worth?

_____

_____

_____

_____

_____

2. What are some positive ways you can think about your physical appearance that can increase your sense of self-worth rather than decrease it?

_____

_____

_____

_____

_____

3. What do you like about your physical appearance? List at least three things. (If it's difficult to come up with a list of positive attributes, aim for a list of features you feel neutral about.)

_____

_____

_____

_____

4. Make a list of things that your body can do that you are grateful for. Start with at least three. (Refer to this list often and add to it whenever you can.)

Chapter Takeaways

- Quality sleep is critical for mental and physical health. Don't skimp on it!
- Making healthy eating choices is one of your best allies when it comes to feeling good physically, which in turn helps you feel confident about yourself.
- Exercise doesn't have to be intimidating. Pick activities you enjoy and start small.
- Love the body that you have right now. Beating yourself up for not looking a certain way is a waste of time.

CHAPTER 8

Prioritizing Mental Health

"Mental health is how we feel and think.
Things that can't really be seen, but that affect us every day and
talking about them can feel difficult.... Sometimes, it's just a
simple conversation that can make things better."

— CATHERINE, DUCHESS OF CAMBRIDGE

M ost of us wouldn't hesitate to schedule an appointment with our doctor for a nasty cold that just won't go away, but we are much less likely to take care of our mental health with the same sense of urgency. Think about it: When you're feeling stressed, overwhelmed, anxious, or depressed, how often do you tell yourself that you just need to work harder to get more organized, be more positive, get stronger, or just be happier? But we know all too well that just willing yourself to be better isn't a guaranteed recipe for health.

In my work with clients, I'll often use the following analogy: If you broke your arm, would you just ignore the pain and try to go about your daily life? Even if you could get through it, the long-term effects would be damaging. Your bone may start to heal itself, but there's no guarantee it will heal properly. It's the same with your mental health. The problem is, too many of us never seek help to have our emotional hurts heal properly. We "get through it," but because they don't heal the right way, the long-term effects can be seriously damaging.

Think about anxiety as an example. Let's say you notice the symptoms: constant worry, feeling restless, trouble concentrating, feeling irritable, sleep issues, muscle tension. You tell yourself to calm down, hoping it will all go away if you just ignore it. But what happens over time? It gets worse, not better. Ignoring the problem instead of tackling it head-on will eventually catch up with you. Like ignoring a broken bone, ignoring mental health can result in terrible consequences over the long term.

Yes, it's easier to see the effects of a physical illness, but that doesn't mean it is more real than any mental health issues. Your mental well-being is just as important. In fact, making your mental health a priority doesn't just help your emotional life, it makes you physically healthier as well. It helps you develop mental resilience as a buffer against the effects of stress, both for the present and in the future. Of course, taking care of your mental health doesn't necessarily mean that you have to seek therapy, but I encourage you not to discount counseling if you are having trouble working through anxiety, depression, or anything else. Thankfully, in recent years our culture has begun to overcome the stigma surrounding mental health, and a good therapist can be a critical component of your long-term well-being.

Mental health is an incredibly broad topic, but for our purposes, we're going to focus on four concrete ways you can invest in your mental well-being: (1) silencing your inner critic; (2) being mindful of social media use; (3) making time for leisure; and (4) believing in yourself.

Silence Your Inner Critic

In Chapter 2, we talked about how toxic listening to your inner critic can be. Your inner critic takes everything that happens to you and turns it into a negative reflection on who you are. Your inner critic tells you that you'll never be enough: good enough, smart enough, thin enough, outgoing enough, lovable enough, etc.

There are three concrete steps you can take to silence your inner critic. The more you practice these steps, the easier it will become, and the better armed you'll be to stop the barrage of negative self-talk that can make daily living so tough.

1. Identify your inner critic's voice.
2. Recognize — and remind yourself — that that voice and everything it tells you is unhealthy, unhelpful, and untrue.
3. Start to reframe your thinking.

Identify Your Inner Critic's Voice

Any thought that is a negative judgment on who you are as a person most likely comes from your inner critic. For example, thoughts like, "I'm a failure as a parent," "No one wants to be friends with me," or "I'll never get the job I want" all come from your inner critic. Learn to recognize these types of thoughts as you're having them. It's all about being mindful of your thoughts and recognizing where they are coming from so you can choose whether or not to believe them, instead of just assuming that they're true.

If you can't recognize your inner critic's influence, you miss out on the chance to choose for yourself what is true about you, your abilities, and your self-worth. When you don't distinguish between rational thoughts and those that come from your inner critic, you fall into the trap of accepting all thoughts you have as true. For example, since the thought "I'm a failure as a friend" occurred to me, I believe that it must be true. But when I recognize the negative, black-and-white tone of that thought, I can identify that it's coming from my inner critic and, therefore, that it's probably not completely true.

Recognize Your Inner Critic's Lies

The thoughts your inner critic feeds you are not helpful, and it's important to recognize that. These thoughts tend to be sweeping judgments about your worthiness as a person. According to your inner critic, you are *always* a failure and *never* good enough. These black-and-white, all-or-nothing types of thoughts are never true. Try to think about it objectively. Are you really "always" a failure at "everything" you do? Of course not. Think about a time when you did succeed at something (and I can guarantee you *have* succeeded at something). Identify something positive you've done or call to mind one of your positive qualities. If this is difficult for you to do on your own, ask someone you're close to and whose opinion you trust. Just one example from your life that challenges these negative thoughts is all you need to show that they are false.

Reframe Your Thoughts

Maybe up until now your inner critic's false statements have guided your life. Or perhaps those thoughts have only come up from time to time. Either way, the first critical step in moving forward is reframing your thinking. It's time to come up with more realistic and true thoughts.

In general, reframing your thoughts means turning from those rooted in blame and judgment to those grounded in the truth of the situation. For example, you can acknowledge, "This is a difficult experience" without blaming yourself for it or letting it color how you perceive yourself as a person. As an example, when you catch yourself thinking, "I'm going to fail this presentation," take a step back. What's the truth of the situation? Consciously decide to tell yourself, "This presentation is challenging and I'll have to work hard to do well, but I have what it takes." You're going to be much more confident walking in to give the presentation when you embrace this way of thinking.

As another example, when you think, "I'll never be able to stick to my exercise routine," flip your thoughts to something more positive — and truer: "I'll take it day by day when it comes to exercise, and I'll try to find exercise activities that I enjoy so that I am more likely to do it." Choosing to think this way makes establishing an exercise routine much more appealing.

It will take practice, but you'll get better and better at recognizing and challenging the lies that your inner critic is feeding you. The better you become at recognizing the lies that come from your inner critic, the freer you'll be to move through life with the grounded confidence you deserve. You won't question whether you're worth the effort or time. You'll be okay with yourself and with what you've been called to do in the world.

Action Plan

1. What are the negative thoughts your inner critic feeds you most
   frequently?

   _____

   _____

   _____

   _____

   _____

2. What are the most common situations in which these thoughts
   occur? (What time of day? Where are you? Who are you with?
   What happened right before? What is about to happen?) Ideally,
   you should start to see a pattern here that can help you better
   identify the times when you might be more prone to those types
   of negative thoughts.

   _____

   _____

   _____

   _____

   _____

3. How can you challenge and reframe each of these thoughts in
   accordance with what's actually true? For each of the negative
   thoughts listed above, write out your response below.

   _____

   _____

   _____

   _____

Be Mindful of Social Media

There's quite a bit of debate out there about the pros and cons of social media, but I tend to think social media itself is pretty neutral. It's how we use it that can either help or hinder personal growth. If you're not careful, it can lead you right into the comparison trap. When you start using your family's, friends', and even strangers' successes as the measuring stick for your own success, you become susceptible to the dangers of the comparison trap. It's easy to fixate on how you measure up to or fall short of other people in your life. And, unfortunately, social media makes it really easy to compare yourself to others.

Your news feed can be an uplifting place, but it can also be a place full of potential pitfalls. For example, after scrolling past a new family photo from your cousin, a hilarious meme, and a cute puppy photo, you see a post from a friend about their latest career accomplishment. Cue the comparison game. Immediately, you start thinking about where you stand in your career and how it compares to your friend's progress, and it isn't a good feeling. You feel like you're behind, you feel inadequate, and you resent your friend's success. All of this comes from a few sentences on a screen.

I know I've fallen prey to the comparison game on social media. When I see all of the amazing work other therapists and writers are doing, if I'm not careful I can start to compare myself to them, and my line of thinking can quickly take a negative turn: *My website isn't as polished*, I think. *My list of speaking engagements isn't as impressive.* And *maybe I'm completely behind in my career and should be more aggressive.* When I fall into this pattern of thinking, I lose focus on what I do and why I do it, and start to feel stressed. In these moments, I forget that, while it's good to be inspired by what others in my field are doing, it isn't healthy to use others' accomplishments as a measure of my own worth.

So, when you see photos from your friend's surprise birthday party, or a post about their recent promotion at work, and start to feel sorry for yourself, remember that the comparison game gets you nowhere. Don't even bother letting your thoughts take you down that path.

This fear is something that comes up often for my clients who are single. "All of my other friends are dating or married and are always off on a date night," they tell me. "I feel like I'm behind on life and am missing out on so much."

It can be easy to take a black-and-white approach here, thinking everyone else is having fun *all the time* and I *never* have fun. Yet social media presents a filtered (no pun intended) view of our friends' lives. No matter how perfect it all looks, your friends have highs and lows in life just like you — they just don't post the lows online. Here it can be helpful to identify recent positive events, social activities, and accomplishments in your own life. This is a great reminder that life is much more nuanced. It's not true that you *never* have fun. You may just need to remind yourself of the fun you've had.

The bottom line is that comparing yourself to others tends to activate your inner critic and the lies it tells you. I love a quote attributed to Theodore Roosevelt, "Comparison is the thief of joy," because it so accurately captures this experience. You may be content and at peace with where you are in life, but once comparison kicks in, that peace and contentment evaporate.

This is why it's important to be mindful of your social media use. Before logging on, ask yourself why you are using it. I used to find myself scrolling through Facebook whenever I was waiting in line, as I was waiting for a client, and when I was bored. I realized that it had become a mindless activity, and I wasn't getting any enjoyment out of it. It had just become a habit: I would unlock my phone and my finger would automatically open my Facebook app without me even thinking about it. I decided to limit my Facebook use by deleting the app from my phone and only accessing it once or twice a day from my computer. It's a strategy that worked really well for me.

While this exact strategy might not work for you, think about how you use social media and how you would like to use social media. If there's a difference, think about what strategies you can use to help use social media the way you want to. Helpful strategies might be limiting how long you use it per day, being mindful of your emotions and reactions to what you see on your news feed, and knowing when it's time to take a break. At least at first, as you're building new habits, you may find it helpful to delete the app from your phone to make it more difficult to access or to take a long-term break from it.

Remember, social media doesn't have to be toxic. It's all about how you use it. Think of it as a tool to help nurture your friendships and stay connected. If all it does is fuel those feelings of not being good enough, it's time to reassess. The good news is that you have the power to decide how you want to use it!

Action Plan

1. How do you use social media? How many times a day do you check it? Do you check from your phone, laptop, tablet, smart watch, all of the above? Which social media sites do you use? Write out your answers below. (There's no right or wrong answer here. Having it all in one place is just a helpful way to start taking ownership of your social media use.)

_____

_____

_____

_____

_____

2. When would you like to use social media each day — for example, after breakfast and after dinner? How long would you like to use social media each time — for example, fifteen minutes?

_____

_____

_____

_____

3. What do you want to get out of social media? Create a plan and strategy for yourself so you know what you're looking for each time you log in. (For example, "I want to celebrate my friends'

successes and be inspired by the creativity I see on my feed.")
Determine what means the most to you, write that down, and try
to make that your social-media strategy every time you log in.
The most important thing is to be intentional about when and
how you're using it.

The Importance of Leisure

Believe it or not, leisure is an essential aspect of your mental well-
being. Too many of us view leisure as nice to have but not essential
to a fulfilling life. After all, if we think our value lies in how busy we
are, then taking time for leisure feels like a waste.

Leisure is far from being a waste of time. Work, even if it's
something you love, is still, well, work. Leisure, on the other hand, is
doing something that brings you joy and fulfillment for its own sake,
not because your boss asked you to or because your paycheck depends
on it. And leisure does not mean mindlessly surfing the internet,
scrolling through social media, or flipping through channels on TV.
Leisure is a much richer concept.

Leisure is intentionally engaging in activities that you enjoy.
Spending time in leisure activities allows you to take a break from
daily obligations and restores your sense of balance, especially after a
sustained period of working. Leisure can reduce stress, increase your
sense of belonging and connection, spark creativity, and positively
contribute to your overall well-being. When you set aside time to
reread your favorite novel, you are making time to enjoy life with
the same focus and concentration that you give your work. When
you make time to meet a friend for coffee, you are saying yes to the
importance and value of healthy friendships.

Leisure activities are an important ingredient in what it means to be fully human. Saying yes to leisure means saying yes to those things that bring you happiness, so it becomes a way for you to acknowledge that you are worth it. You are worth the time and attention it takes to spend time in leisure because it brings you happiness.

Engaging in leisure activities, whether that means playing sports, enjoying the arts, or sitting outside in the sunshine, is a great way to manage stress. I personally find drawing and watercolor painting very relaxing. I don't plan to quit my day job and become an artist, but it helps me decompress after a stressful and busy day.

How much time do you make for leisure in your day? Often, when I work with clients to develop a self-care plan, they'll tell me that they don't have time for leisure activities. If you also feel this way, don't be discouraged: enjoying leisure doesn't have to take many hours — or even a full hour — and it doesn't need to be a complicated activity. Fitting some time for leisure into your day could mean just fifteen minutes to read a chapter or two of your favorite book, taking a quick walk around the block, or writing a note to a friend. Incorporating leisure into your day is completely possible. It might not be the same time every day, but try to set aside fifteen minutes to do something you love. Even those few minutes can make a significant and positive difference in your stress levels.

The trick is to change the way you think about and value time for leisure. Instead of leisure being an "if I have time today" activity, try to think of it as a priority in your day. Identify a few leisure activities that you really enjoy. Then, set aside time each day (beginning with fifteen minutes) to fit at least one of those activities in. When you give yourself the chance to do something purely because you enjoy it, you will find it easier to make it a priority in your day.

Action Plan

1. What are the top two or three leisure activities you would like to make time for, starting now?

_____

_____

_____

2. Make it happen: When do you want to engage in these leisure activities? For how long? Be realistic about what you can commit to each week, but try to challenge yourself.

Believe in Yourself

How do you think about yourself and your place in the world? Do you believe wholeheartedly in your abilities and in your right to be taken seriously? Or are you constantly battling feelings of self-doubt? Sadly, many of us are paralyzed by self-doubt. The more we let it fester, the more we doubt that others value our company and talents, and we lose confidence in our ability to do well, whether at work, in a relationship, or with our families. So how do you prevent self-doubt from sabotaging your life?

Similar to silencing your inner critic, dialing down your self-doubt means reminding yourself of your inherent worthiness, your talents (everyone has them!), and being okay with making occasional mistakes. Sometimes, it can feel a bit like "fake it till you make it," but this is how you arrive at being able to own your place in the world. Being confident in yourself and your abilities does not mean thinking you are better than everyone else. It means acknowledging that you have something great to offer to the world. When you act with confidence, people respond positively to it.

How do you silence self-doubt and fuel self-confidence? It may feel a little funny at first, but I strongly recommend you start by listing your positive qualities, your accomplishments, and anything about you that you are particularly proud of. Keep that list someplace where you can easily access it: on a Post-it note at work, on your phone, or on a bathroom mirror at home. Refer to this list whenever you feel like you aren't good enough, and add to it every time you accomplish something you are proud of.

You can also adapt the strategies used for silencing your inner critic. When you are not feeling confident, your thoughts are probably running along these lines: "Why would anyone want to listen to me?" "I don't know if I'll do a good job at this." "Am I the right person for this? Isn't there someone who would be better?" Challenge these thoughts. Remind yourself of all the great qualities you do have. You don't have to be perfect or the best at anything, but you do have what it takes, whether at work, in a relationship, or managing your home. And it's okay to ask for help.

Your confidence will continue to grow as you work on your self-care plan. It won't happen overnight, but it will slowly change over time the more your practice and allow yourself to persevere, especially when you feel like giving up. As you take care of your mental health, you'll start to feel the difference.

Action Plan

1. When do you most often experience self-doubt? Write down the most frequent thoughts of self-doubt you have.

_____

_____

_____

_____

_____

2. Make a list of your accomplishments and positive qualities. You can do that here, or write it on a separate sheet of paper and put it somewhere you can easily refer to when you are hit with a wave of self-doubt. (If you're having trouble, ask someone you trust to help you come up with a list.)

_____

_____

_____

_____

_____

_____

_____

Chapter Takeaways

- Learn to recognize your inner critic's voice by keeping an eye out for thoughts that are black and white, always/never, and negative in tone.
- Reframe your inner critic's thoughts so that they more accurately reflect what is really happening in your life.
- Be mindful of when, how, and why you use social media so that it stays an uplifting and positive environment.
- Make leisure a daily priority, even if it's only fifteen minutes a day.
- Banish self-doubt by making a list of your accomplishments and positive qualities, and refer back to it often.

CHAPTER 9

Managing Emotions

"Mental pain is less dramatic than physical pain, but it is more common and also more hard to bear. The frequent attempt to conceal mental pain increases the burden: it is easier to say 'My tooth is aching' than to say 'My heart is broken.'"

— C. S. Lewis, Christian apologist

E motions tend to get a bad rap in our world. From childhood, many of us learned to "control" our emotions, which turned into avoiding the way we really feel in difficult situations. We learned that feeling too happy or too sad means that we aren't in control of ourselves. We also learned that there are "good" emotions and "bad" emotions. It's okay to be excited or happy (but not too happy), but it's not okay to feel sad, scared, or angry, so we learned to work hard to ignore those feelings.

Because some emotions can be scary, we figure out ways to ignore or bury them. Either we pretend that we don't feel them, or we choose to feel some and not others. This can have terrible consequences for our happiness, our mental and emotional health, and our relationships. Instead, we need to recognize our real emotions in any given situation, identify why we feel this way, and then take practical steps to address this emotion so it doesn't lead to problems in the long run.

There's no reason to be afraid of your emotions. Actually, they are a powerful clue to how we think about ourselves, our lives, our relationships, our goals, and our fears. Emotional awareness (being able to label the emotion you are experiencing and identify why you are feeling that way) is a valuable tool that helps us identify our personal needs so we can take proper care of ourselves.

It probably won't surprise you then to learn that taking care of ourselves emotionally has a positive long-term impact on mental, emotional, physical, and spiritual health. It's a critical part of any self-care routine. Let's take a look at six effective and relatively simple ways you can increase your emotional awareness and live a freer, more authentic life.

1. "Feel" your feelings.
2. Harness your emotions for growth.
3. Live in the present moment.
4. Take a deep breath.
5. Give thanks.
6. Write it down.

Let Yourself "Feel" Your Feelings

Being able to name the emotion you are experiencing is incredibly powerful when it comes to self-improvement and making decisions. What we feel gives us a strong clue about what we think and believe about certain situations. Here's an example I frequently use with my clients: Imagine you have a coworker who says hello every time they pass your desk as they leave for the day. One day, they walk past you without even acknowledging your existence. How would you feel in this situation? It's possible you would feel hurt by what you perceive as a snub.

If you don't stop right then and acknowledge that you are feeling hurt and confused, you won't be able to think through the reasons why you are feeling the way you do. Acknowledging the feelings allows you to tease apart the truth from your own assumptions. Think about this example: Does believing that your coworker is mad at you make it true? Not necessarily. What's more likely is that your coworker merely forgot, was distracted by something, or simply didn't see you. Giving yourself the chance to identify what you are feeling and to think about why you are feeling that way allows you to discern whether or not your emotions fit with the situation, and to deal with your feelings accordingly.

We often think we should experience certain emotions and not others. We tell ourselves that we shouldn't be embarrassed, worried, sad, or even excited at times. Then, when we do feel these "forbidden" emotions, we criticize ourselves for feeling the wrong way. Here's the good news: emotions in themselves are neither good nor bad. They are clues to our thoughts, our reactions, and sometimes to the deeper realities going on in our minds, hearts, and souls.

From now on, instead of labeling emotions as "good" or "bad," try harnessing them to help you respond to situations. Knowing what you are feeling and why you are feeling that way gives you power over your actions, rather than blindsiding you when you explode in anger or find yourself worrying excessively about something. Get comfortable with acknowledging your emotions instead of ignoring them or brushing them aside. When you have emotional awareness, the mystery behind how you respond and react to situations vanishes. Knowledge is power. So, go ahead and feel *all* of your feelings.

Action Plan

1. What are some of your implicit assumptions about good and bad emotions? Are these assumptions actually true?

---

2. If they aren't true, what's a better and more accurate way to think of emotions?

_____

_____

_____

_____

_____

_____

Harness Your Emotions for Growth

Being able to label your emotions gives you valuable clues to help guide you through the ups and downs of life. In particular, emotional awareness actually helps us make better decisions, which has a huge impact on our growth — personally, professionally, and spiritually. A great Catholic thinker and leader, Saint Ignatius (founder of the Jesuits), put together a list of rules to help guide decision-making, using our emotions among other factors. His focus was on discerning the will of God, and we can apply his principles to just about any area of our life.

When you are trying to figure out the best way to act in a certain situation, your emotions can help discern what action is best to take. For example, if you are in a relationship and your significant other constantly puts you down, you are likely to feel ashamed of who you are. This feeling of being ashamed can help you discern what action is best for you to take. If your partner is pointing out something that's true, you can take the necessary steps to grow and overcome the bad habits your partner sees. On the other hand, if your partner constantly puts you down to make himself (or herself) feel better, your feeling of shame can help take steps to reclaim your self-worth by leaving that unhealthy relationship.

This is a complex topic, but we'll cover enough here to give you an idea of how your emotions are useful. If you are interested in learning more about Saint Ignatius's method (called discernment of spirits), reach out to a trusted Catholic spiritual leader or priest who can provide you with direction in this area. You might also want to check out the recommended books in Appendix A.

Action Plan

1. What's a decision that you are facing right now? How are you feeling about it?

_____

_____

_____

_____

_____

2. How can you use your emotions to help guide you in your decision using the strategy described above?

_____

_____

_____

_____

Live in the Present Moment

Stop for a moment and think about the last time you worried about something. Maybe it was just a few minutes ago ("How am I ever going to start making these lifestyle changes?"). Or perhaps it was a day or two ago. But my guess is that you've worried about something recently. We all worry, from small things like traffic or what to eat for lunch, to bigger things like whether to leave that job, move, or end a relationship. Yet worrying can trap us in a never-ending loop instead of giving us the boost we need to take action.

Worrying holds you back from being your most authentic self, because worry says that you should live in fear and regret — neither of which foster self-love. It doesn't matter if you're worrying about something that happened in the past or about something that hasn't yet happened, it doesn't accomplish anything productive. Instead, it drains and paralyzes you. The past has already happened and can't be changed, so it's useless to wish you could go back and change your actions. And the future hasn't happened yet — and isn't even guaranteed to happen.

When you find yourself worrying, it's helpful to ask yourself whether there's any action you can take *right now* to help solve that worry. If there is something you can do about it, do it. If there isn't anything you can do right now, then remind yourself that worrying isn't going to accomplish anything. Remember, in the Gospel, Jesus tells us not to worry: "Do not be anxious about tomorrow, for tomorrow will be anxious for itself" (Mt 6:34).

His words give us the clue for avoiding worry. It sounds really simple, but it can be very difficult: it's living in the present moment. This is one of the most powerful and effective things you can do to combat worry. When you focus on the present, you are completely engaged in what is happening right here, right now. You are living in the moment. And when you're living in the moment, there's no room for worries to push their way in.

This type of living in the present is different from being reckless or impulsive. It's not ignoring the consequences your actions today will have on tomorrow. Instead, it's about valuing what's happening in the moment because it grounds you in reality. When you are aware of what's happening right now, you are present in the world where God has placed you that very moment. And that's a powerful experience. While you should take prudent steps to prepare for the future or to take responsibility for past actions, the only place you can be fully alive is in the present moment. You can't live in the past. You can't live in the future. But you can live right now.

Another word for living in the present moment is mindfulness. You may have heard this term before, and perhaps you automatically associate it with New Age practices, but it actually has deep roots in Christianity. For example, practicing Saint Ignatius's discernment of spirits requires us to be mindful of what we are experiencing that very moment. Prayer requires us to be really present so we can focus on God — this is especially true in Eucharistic adoration, where we need to be present so we can focus on Jesus, who is truly present in the monstrance. Praying the Rosary requires us to be fully present as we repeat the Hail Mary and hold the rosary beads between our fingers.

Mindfulness has a lot of power to combat worry, and there's plenty of research to back this idea up. Research shows that practicing mindfulness is associated with reduced rumination, stress reduction, increased focus, and reduced symptoms of depression and anxiety.[10] What makes mindfulness even more appealing in addition to these benefits is that it is relatively simple to incorporate into your daily routine.

Pause and Be Present

One of the easiest ways to practice mindfulness is to pause for just a minute to notice what is happening around you.

- Take a deep breath and use all five of your senses to help you take in the present.
- Look around you. What do you see? Are there people moving about, birds flying, or even just a stack of papers on your desk?
- What do you hear? Maybe you hear the sounds of people talking, a printer that's running, or the wind blowing through the trees.
- Are there any smells you notice? Perhaps someone just brewed a pot of coffee, or maybe it just rained and you smell that familiar scent of wet leaves.
- Is there anything you can feel? This could be feeling your back propped up against your chair as you read this book, the texture of the shirt you're wearing, or the smooth feel of the pen you're holding at work.
- What can you taste? Take a slow sip of water, tea, or coffee and notice the taste of your drink, along with the sensation of drinking and swallowing.

That's it — you just practiced mindfulness. See how easy it can be? When you pause, even for a minute, to focus on what is happening around you, you give yourself permission to live in the present.

Action Plan

1. How do you think you could benefit from practicing living in the present moment?

2. What do you worry about most frequently?

3. Go through each of your worries and identify whether or not there is action you can take to help you proactively deal with your worries right now. If there's no action to be taken, note on the list that worrying isn't going to accomplish anything.

Take a Deep Breath

I frequently use deep breathing in my daily life, whether it's to help decompress after an emotionally charged session or transition to focus on the needs of the next client. I've also used deep breathing to help me manage any pre-exam or interview jitters I've had in my career. This is a simple, powerful way to manage your emotions, and it can be done anywhere, anytime.

This type of breathing focuses exclusively on the act of breathing slowly. There are many different versions of deep breathing, but a good starting point is to breathe in slowly through your nose for four seconds, hold your breath for four seconds, and breathe out slowly through your mouth for four seconds. Pause and then slowly breathe in again.

As you breathe in and out, focus on how it feels: breathe in, filling your lungs with air and expanding your diaphragm. As you breathe out, focus on what it feels like as the air leaves your lungs and goes through your mouth. Your goal is to focus on the physical sensation of breathing and not on the thoughts that may pop up in your brain. If you start to get distracted, calmly redirect your focus to your breathing without berating yourself for getting distracted.

If you still feel intimidated, there are quite a few excellent free smartphone apps that can help guide you through deep-breathing exercises. I am personally a big fan of the Calm app, which offers several deep-breathing options as well as some relaxation scripts you can use when you are trying to fall asleep. I also recommend this app to clients, and they've given me positive feedback.

Action Plan

1. Make a plan for the situations when you are going to practice deep breathing to regain some control of your emotions. Write down the top two or three situations you frequently encounter where this practice could be helpful to you.

Give Thanks

Practicing gratitude is an uplifting and easy way to practice living in the present. When you are filled with regret for something that happened in the past or are worried about something that might happen in the future, the positive things that are happening in your life right now fade to the background. Intentionally practicing gratitude throughout the day can help combat any tendency you may have to default to worrying.

Research on the benefits of gratitude shows that intentionally noticing the good things happening in your life can increase your motivation to achieve goals, energize you to pursue them, and increase feelings of connectedness to others.[11] Research has also demonstrated that people who practice gratitude experience better mental health.[12]

When I talk about practicing gratitude with my clients, I encourage them to start by simply making a list of what they are grateful for. The list doesn't have to be long. You could begin with three things you are grateful for today. Feel free to list the big things that you are grateful for (health, job, family, etc.) along with the little things (a sunny day, an extra hour to sleep in, a compliment from someone).

For example, my own gratitude list always includes a travel mug that keeps my coffee piping hot for a few hours. I tend to sip coffee slowly, and without this mug my coffee gets ice cold too quickly and I'm left to debate whether to microwave it (again) or brew a fresh cup. This travel mug has been a game changer. It's not a flashy or big thing to be grateful for, but it makes my day a little bit easier and brighter.

Action Plan

1. Go ahead and start a gratitude list right now. List three to five things you are grateful for today.

_____

_____

_____

_____

_____

Write It Down

Journaling is another helpful way to deal with worry and to practice mindfulness. Spending just a few minutes each day processing the events of the day, or any other concerns or experiences, comes with research-backed benefits such as reduced stress and anxiety.[13]

People frequently think of journaling as a preteen girl's "Dear Diary" exercise, but it is so much more than that. Journaling can help you process, connect the dots, or problem solve things that are on your mind. My clients who journal will often bring in what they've written to share with me so we can discuss it together. But sharing what you write isn't a requirement for successful journaling. What matters is that you use it as a tool to help you realistically address concerns, deal with them, and move past them so you can stop living with constant worry. Spending ten minutes writing down anything that's on your mind can be beneficial.

Action Plan

1. How do you think you could benefit from journaling? Make a commitment to journal a certain number of days per week for a month and see what benefits you experience. Write down the days and times you plan to devote just ten minutes to journaling.

_____

_____

_____

_____

Chapter Takeaways

- Emotions aren't something to be afraid of! Acknowledge and use them to help guide you in making decisions.
- Worrying about what happened in the past or about what will happen in the future does not accomplish anything. It just drains you. Learn to recognize worry and stop it in its tracks.
- Pressing pause on a busy day, even for a minute, in order to use your five senses and take in the world around you is a valuable way to make yourself a priority.
- Literally just taking a breath can make a huge difference in the way you handle stress.
- Being thankful is not a once-yearly occurrence when you're sitting around the table with your family at Thanksgiving. Practicing gratitude is a powerful year-round mood booster.
- Putting pen to paper can help you gain insight into what's happening in your life that you might not have otherwise had. Try it and see!

CHAPTER 10

Nurturing Relationships

"Every one of us needs to show how much we care for each other and, in the process, care for ourselves."

— PRINCESS DIANA

Healthy relationships are not only an important ingredient for living an authentic life but also an important part of self-care. Our relationships and how we interact with others reflects how we think and feel about ourselves. When we truly believe in our own self-worth, this shines in our relationships with others. They can sense it, see it, and respond positively to it. Authentic confidence can only come from a deeply rooted sense of our own inherent worth. And that requires the courage to be okay with taking an honest assessment of the things we believe about ourselves that might be preventing us from living out healthy, Christian relationships. In this chapter, we'll take a look at some of the things that might be having a negative effect on our relationships.

Whether it's relationships involving romance, friendships, work, or family, these connections can be deeply fulfilling and impact our emotional, physical, and spiritual well-being. Healthy relationships are sources of encouragement, wisdom, guidance, and support during tough times.

It's probably no surprise, then, that unhealthy relationships have the opposite effect. What does an unhealthy relationship look like? It's any relationship that requires us to make compromises and concessions in order to "earn" respect or love from the other person. It's easy to fall into the trap of basing our self-worth on how others view us, whether family members, friends, coworkers, or significant others. When we allow this habit to become deeply ingrained, we open ourselves to unhealthy, potentially damaging relationships.

Unhealthy relationships can decrease our sense of self-worth and confidence in our abilities. And, unfortunately, these relationships can occur in just about any area of your life. It could be an overbearing boss at work, a coworker who rarely contributes, a family member who is constantly critical, a romantic partner who blames you for everything that goes wrong in the relationship, or a friend who is always asking for big favors but never offers to help you. These types of relationships demand more and more time and energy until you feel stretched thin and drained.

If the people in your life consistently send you the message — either explicitly or implicitly — that you're worthless and unlovable, over time you will start to internalize that message and believe it. Instead of helping you be the best version of yourself, these relationships drag you deeper into damaging cycles of self-doubt and self-loathing.

The truth is, no other human being can define us or give us our self-worth. God created us in his image and likeness, and *that's* where our inherent worth comes from. Christian relationships are centered on the belief that all of us are worthy and deserve to be treated as such. This means you should expect to be treated that way. Healthy relationships start with a healthy relationship with yourself.

The good news is: You are not powerless. You can foster and maintain healthy relationships while still taking good care of yourself. The key is to know the ingredients of a healthy relationship, whether with a family member, friend, significant other, or coworker. Deeply believing in your own self-worth, identifying and setting boundaries, and making time for the people who are important in your life are essential practices for cultivating healthy relationships.

Setting Boundaries

Being okay with yourself means believing that you deserve to be treated with respect and that you don't have to accept anything less. And, believe me, you will run into situations where other people won't give you the respect you deserve unless you demand it. This can happen at work, with family, and in any relationship.

When I was beginning my graduate externship training to be a therapist, I encountered clients who were skeptical of my ability to help them. The fact that I was "in training," combined with the fact that I look much younger than I am, led some people to ask: "Are you sure you can help me? What do you know about my problems?" This could have been really discouraging to someone just starting out in the field and trying to build confidence in newly learned skills, but, luckily, I had a wise, experienced, and encouraging supervisor who helped me stand up for myself and my abilities so that I would earn my clients' respect and develop a positive working relationship with each one of them. I could have let their doubt get to me, but I chose instead (with my supervisor's wise help) to enforce the boundary and belief that I had something valuable to offer them as a therapist.

This is an example of setting boundaries, and it's a skill we all need to develop in interactions with others, not just professionally but personally. Identifying and setting boundaries is one of the most powerful tools for fostering healthy relationships. Boundaries encourage mutual respect and provide the context that frees you to be authentic and vulnerable without fearing that others may take advantage of you.

What does it mean to be "taken advantage of"? For most of us, it happens in little ways, such as when coworkers push their work onto you, when your significant other ignores your requests to help with housework, or when your friend just assumes you will make the traffic-filled drive to the airport to pick them up. Why is this a problem? Because feeling taken advantage of breeds resentment, and resentment makes it really hard to live a happy and fulfilling life.

So, to make sure our relationships aren't filling us with resentment, we need to get good at setting boundaries. What exactly are boundaries, you might be wondering? Think of boundaries as what you are okay with and not okay with in any type of relationship.

Just as a fence keeps out what you don't want (like your neighbor's dogs who dig holes in your lawn) and keeps in what you do want (like your kids who can play freely without running into the street), boundaries give you the freedom to foster the good and help keep out the bad in relationships.

Boundaries encompasses a many-layered concept, and it starts with personal boundaries. For me, as a therapist and a writer, I don't keep the traditional nine-to-five work hours, so I'm pretty much in charge of setting my own schedule. On one hand, this is a fantastic privilege, because it allows me a lot of flexibility to fit meetings in, schedule clients, run errands, and write. I love this aspect of my working life. But if I'm not careful, I can be fully booked from early morning until late in the evening, leaving me no time for basic self-care — eating an actual lunch (instead of a protein bar between sessions), exercising, or spending quality time with the people closest to me. Setting a schedule for myself and maintaining strict boundaries for when I am available for meetings, when I see clients, and when I write, has helped me stay balanced on a daily basis. An occasional busy day is okay, but when every day is booked solid, it becomes a recipe for stress and not for success.

Emotional boundaries are also an important ingredient in healthy relationships. While most of us know what to share and what not to share with others, sometimes strong emotions in a relationship can confuse our boundaries and lead to trouble. Emotional boundaries can be blurred when we share our feelings with someone who has not earned that privilege. They can also become blurred when we idealize others and grow too attached to them, even if it's not reciprocated. And this can happen in a variety of relationships whether involving dating, work, friendship, or mentoring. Idealizing another person blinds us to the fact that he or she is human and imperfect, which can leave us feeling betrayed and disappointed when we are inevitably let down.

Physical boundaries also play a role in healthy relationships, no matter what type of relationship it is. At its simplest, most of us know instinctively what physical contact we are okay with and not okay with. Each of us is in charge of our own personal space. We all have different levels of comfort when it comes to personal space, and there isn't a right or wrong answer when it comes to defining your own space. Take the time to think about what you are okay with and what you aren't, and then think about how you will enforce those boundaries.

Another important aspect of setting boundaries is learning to say no. Many of us struggle with this. We want to be able to say "Yes!" any time our friends or loved ones reach out. Often, we're even a little afraid to say no. Yet when we feel compelled to say yes to every request, we aren't doing ourselves or anyone else any favors. When you're afraid to say no, you open yourself up to a lot of hurt and resentment, which seriously impacts relationships and quality of life.

Remember: You are the one who sets and enforces your boundaries. No one else can do that for you. Don't be afraid to own the fact that you are worth the effort of setting boundaries.

Action Plan

1. Identify any relationships you have that you think could benefit from boundaries. Who is the relationship with? Where specifically would you like to set boundaries?

_____

_____

_____

_____

_____

2. Identify how you would like to enforce your boundaries within each of these relationships. Be as concrete as possible.

_____

_____

_____

_____

3. What are some fears you have about setting boundaries? How can you address and challenge those fears and make a rationale for cultivating boundaries despite these fears?

_____

_____

_____

_____

_____

_____

4. What are some situations in which you could benefit from being comfortable with saying no? Next time you encounter one of these situations, make an effort to be brave and say no!

_____

_____

_____

_____

_____

_____

Making Time for the People Who Matter Most

Setting personal boundaries allows you to invest time and energy into those things that should take priority in your life, especially relationships. Family, friends, and significant others are key ingredients in a happy and healthy life, and maintaining these relationships is an important aspect of self-care.

Your family and friends are the ones who can point out when you are struggling to be okay with yourself. They can encourage and motivate you to focus on self-care when you don't feel like it. If you have these healthy relationships in your life, hold on to them. Sadly, I have learned in my work as a therapist that not everyone is blessed with deep, lasting friendships. But the good news is that even if these types of relationships are currently missing in your life, there are things you can do to build them. Finding like-minded people through friends, acquaintances, and social groups (whether through your church, gym, office, or other organizations) can be a great place to start. All it takes is being intentional about seeking out a few kindred spirits and a little effort to help those friendships grow.

Fostering relationships with family and friends isn't always easy. It requires some creativity when you have a busy schedule. Honoring obligations, including work, is a necessary and important part of life, but relationships are even more important. Yet it often seems like the work side of life commandeers all of our time, leaving very little for the more important things in life. This is especially tough for working parents. Balance is important, but we shouldn't be too rigid in the way we think about it.

Our lives can't always be perfectly split between work and personal life, but we need to be mindful of making time to invest in relationships and self-care. Here are some things I've found that work well to help cultivate healthy relationships despite a busy schedule.

- Standing coffee dates
- Quick phone calls to check in
- Sharing an article or social media post that made me think of my friend or family member
- Writing a quick note and mailing it (who doesn't love to get "snail mail"?)
- Asking a friend to join me to run errands so we can check items off our to-do list and still spend time together
- Creating regular work dates with friends who also have flexible work schedules

I encourage you to think about the relationships you want to maintain the most and to come up with some creative ways to reach out and spend time with the people you love.

Action Plan

1. List the relationships that are a priority in your life.

_____

_____

_____

_____

_____

_____

2. What are some challenges you face with cultivating and maintaining these relationships?

_____

_____

_____

_____

_____

3. List creative and specific ways you would like to stay in touch with your family and friends even when life is busy. (Refer to what you wrote for number two above and try to address these with your solutions here.)

_____

_____

_____

_____

_____

4. Do you wish you had more friends? What might be holding you back from having fulfilling friendships? What are some positive steps you can take, starting today, to reach out and make connections with people?

Chapter Takeaways

- Healthy relationships make us better people and boundaries provide the structure you need to cultivate and maintain those relationships.
- Saying no is a powerful tool when it comes to fostering healthy relationships and keeping you from becoming overwhelmed by an overbooked calendar and to-do list.
- Keeping in touch with family and friends is counterintuitive but essential in times of stress. Be intentional and creative about it!

CHAPTER 11

Making Time for Prayer

"We need to find God, and he cannot be found in noise and restlessness. God is the friend of silence. See how nature — trees, flowers, grass — grows in silence; see the stars, the moon and the sun, how they move in silence…. We need silence to be able to touch souls."

— Saint Teresa of Calcutta

Your relationship with God is the foundation of your life and well-being. More than anything else, it gives you the "why" for living your life authentically. Your spiritual life informs your physical, mental, emotional, and relational life. It guides how you approach relationships, it provides a strong reason for caring for your health, and it can give you the motivation to stay true to investing in your well-being when the going gets tough.

Because of this, cultivating a strong prayer life — which is essential in its own right — is a critical part of self-care. Prayer and other spiritual practices are beneficial to our overall well-being, and research supports this claim. Individuals who report having strong religious beliefs also reported lower levels of anxiety and depression, lower blood pressure, and a better immune system.[14] Other research shows that contemplative prayer increases your ability to concentrate and quiets the part of your brain that is focused on the self.[15] And studies show that prayer can help increase self-control as well.[16]

Even more importantly, conversation with God through prayer reminds us of God's love for us and strengthens our belief in our inherent dignity and worth. It helps us see ourselves the way God sees us, as loved beings created in his image. It helps us to begin to believe that his love is freely given and not dependent on anything we do (whether those actions are positive or negative). The more we can see and believe in God's love for us, the more we will be able to love ourselves as we are, and to treat ourselves with love and care.

Most of us know that prayer, meditation, and silence should be an important part of our lives. Yet for some reason, when life gets stressful, prayer falls by the wayside. Sometimes, it feels like the only way to press pause and focus on your spiritual health is by going off and living as a hermit. Since very few of us can actually drop our obligations and move to the desert (plus, I think I would get lonely!), we have to figure out ways to make spiritual practices a priority while still honoring our other commitments.

When it comes to taking care of your spiritual well-being, your goal is to find a way to cultivate an authentic spiritual life within the structure of your life *as it is right now.*

Your spiritual practices don't have to be perfect. If you aim for perfect, you'll only get discouraged. Instead of aiming for the perfect prayer life, try to think of your spiritual life as cultivating a friendship with someone who cares deeply about you. You will always have that friendship, even though it will look different depending on what season of life you are in. For example, if you are a young professional with no family responsibilities, weekly adoration could be a wonderful way to cultivate your spiritual life. But if you are a new parent juggling child-care with work, you might be limited to fifteen minutes of prayer in the morning, before the kids wake up. If you work outside the home, listening to a spiritual podcast or a reflection on the Gospels on your commute might be the best way to work some meditation into your day. The key is recognizing the limitations imposed by the season of life you are in and coming up with creative ways to work around those limitations to build a consistent prayer life.

Maintaining spiritual health takes time, attention, and

commitment. In general, it is helpful to think of the time you spend in spiritual practices as time invested in building your friendship with God. We make time for friends and family despite busy schedules, and we should do the same for God. Thinking about prayer this way is really helpful for me. When I'm tempted to skip reading the daily Gospel reflection I subscribe to by email, I try to remember that it's time spent deepening my friendship with God. I definitely recognize when it's been way too long since I last spoke to one of my friends, and I should feel the same way when it's been too long since my last conversation with God.

The way to take care of your spiritual health will be unique to you. You know yourself, your schedule, and your spiritual needs best. The one element that is consistent for all of us is making the time — and then committing to that. Whether it's ten minutes of Scripture reading every morning or thirty minutes of quiet prayer during your lunch hour, find the time that works for you, and make that a priority every day.

Here are some suggestions to get you started, no matter how busy your life may be:

- Subscribe to a daily Gospel reading and reflection. (I recommend Bishop Robert Barron's at wordonfire.org or Blessed is She's daily reflections.)
- Set aside at least fifteen minutes each day for prayer. Find a quiet spot in your house, a local church, or a local adoration chapel, and commit to that time, even if you just sit in silence with God.
- Find spiritual podcasts or radio programs you can listen to on your morning commute. (I recommend podcasts form Fr. Mike Schmitz or The Catholic Feminist, but there are many other options as well.)
- Read (or listen) to spiritual books.
- Join a weekly Bible study or a spiritual book club. Contact your church to see what is available to you.
- If you are Catholic (as I am), I highly recommend participating in the sacraments regularly, especially confession.

Action Plan

1.   What holds you back from taking care of your spiritual health?

_____

_____

_____

_____

_____

_____

2.   What time of day are you most fresh? Consider spending just fifteen minutes during this time to pray, meditate, or journal.

_____

_____

_____

_____

3.   What are some roadblocks to your prayer life based on the season of life you are in?

_____

_____

_____

_____

_____

_____

4. How can you work around these roadblocks so they don't hold you back spiritually?

_____

_____

_____

_____

_____

5. Jot down a list of three spiritual practices you would like to commit to on a daily or weekly basis. Identify what day, what time, and where you'd like to do these.

_____

_____

_____

_____

_____

Chapter Takeaways
- Cultivating your spiritual health is like staying in touch with and deepening your relationship with a friend — in this case, with the best friend you could ever have.
- Be creative about incorporating spiritual practices into your busy schedule.
- Don't aim for spiritual perfection, but for commitment. Keep trying each day, even when it's difficult. What matters most is that you are always aiming to deepen your relationship with God.

CHAPTER 12

How to Build a Self-Care Plan

"It is not the mountain we conquer but ourselves."

— Edmund Hillary, adventurer
(first man to climb Mount Everest)

Now that you've had a chance to take the Self-Care Assessment (and if you haven't already, go back and take it!), and we've examined the different areas of self-care, it's time to put together your unique self-care plan. This is the exciting part, where you get to put together a personalized plan for taking charge of your well-being.

As tempting as it might be to start making every change all at once, it's important to start with small, easy-to-implement changes that are doable and sustainable. Your goal here is to set yourself up for success, which means being honest with yourself and making changes that you can really commit to. For example, maybe you'd like to start focusing on healthy eating. While you may be tempted to completely clean out your fridge and pantry and start from scratch, you might find yourself abandoning your plan after a few days or weeks because it was too much of a radical change. Instead, try focusing on one meal at a time and gradually build up from there.

To set achievable goals, try following the SMART strategy.[17] SMART is frequently used by project planners in the corporate world and by counselors. The acronym stands for **S**pecific, **M**easurable, **A**ttainable, **R**ealistic, **T**ime frame. Sticking with these attributes has been shown to increase the likelihood of making achievable goals. For example, "I want to exercise more" is much vaguer than "I am going to use the rowing machine at the gym for thirty minutes on Monday, Tuesday, and Thursday at 7:30 a.m." Try to keep the SMART guidelines in mind as you set goals. Describe your goal in specific terms and in a way that is realistic and attainable. If you don't have a regular exercise routine right now, committing to a thirty-minute walk in your neighborhood is much more realistic and attainable than running the local 5k in two weeks.

Don't let yourself become overwhelmed as you make these self-care goals. You'll only be incorporating a few at a time, and you won't (and shouldn't) be tackling all of them at once. Remember, you are aiming for lasting lifestyle changes, not a temporary fix. This isn't a crash diet. Your Self-Care Action Plan will give you a new way of living and a new way of interacting with the world. It's not about making surface-level changes. It's about making a fundamental change in the way you think about yourself. Having the patience to start with small changes will help you build confidence that it truly is okay to start with yourself, and you will see the payoff in your life.

Go back and look through the notes you took throughout the second part of this book. These notes will help guide you as you discern what goals you should set. Some of your notes will probably already have some suggested goals and steps mapped out. If these still resonate, just transfer them over to the Action Plan below. Add in any other goals that come to mind as you review your notes, keeping SMART in mind.

You will see below that there is space for five goals for each area of self-care. You might have fewer or you might have more, but I encourage you to map out three to five goals for each section. You might even want to consider ranking them in order of the easiest one to implement to the most challenging. Below each goal, you will see space to indicate how frequently you would like to implement it, how long it will last, and where you will accomplish this goal. For example, if you'd like to start journaling, you might say you want to journal daily for ten minutes at your kitchen table with a cup of coffee. Or maybe you'd like to schedule a phone call with an out-of-town friend once a month for about twenty minutes while you're out walking around your neighborhood. Keep in mind that the simpler the goal, the easier it will be to make it a lasting change.

Go ahead and fill out this Action Plan, and be sure to use a pencil. That way, you can easily refine and edit it in the future. In fact, I encourage you to revisit your plan every few weeks to assess how you are doing and to determine whether you need to tweak it. Keep it in an easily accessible place such as on a nightstand, a desk, or another prominent place so you will see it daily. Remember, forming a new habit takes time, so it's important to be consistent each day with your Self-Care Action Plan to increase the likelihood of long-term success.

There are sample plans in Appendix 1 if you'd like to see some ideas for what an Action Plan might look like. But keep in mind that it's okay if your plan looks different. In fact, it should probably be different since we all have different needs, concerns, and personal goals.

Personalized Self-Care Action Plan

1. PHYSICAL HEALTH

Goal #1: _____

_____

_____

Frequency:　Daily　Weekly　Monthly　Other:_____

Duration: _____

Location: _____

Goal #2: _____

_____

_____

Frequency:　Daily　Weekly　Monthly　Other:_____

Duration: _____

Location: _____

Goal #3: _____

_____

_____

Frequency:　Daily　Weekly　Monthly　Other:_____

Duration: _____

Location: _____

Goal #4: _____

_____

_____

Frequency: Daily   Weekly   Monthly   Other:_____

Duration: _____

Location: _____

Goal #5: _____

_____

_____

Frequency: Daily   Weekly   Monthly   Other:_____

Duration: _____

Location: _____

Goal #6: _____

_____

_____

Frequency: Daily   Weekly   Monthly   Other:_____

Duration: _____

Location: _____

2. MENTAL HEALTH

Goal #1: _____

_____

_____

Frequency: Daily   Weekly   Monthly   Other:_____

Duration: _____

Location: _____

Goal #2: _____

_____

_____

Frequency: Daily   Weekly   Monthly   Other:_____

Duration: _____

Location: _____

Goal #3: _____

_____

_____

Frequency: Daily   Weekly   Monthly   Other:_____

Duration: _____

Location: _____

Goal #4: _____

_____

_____

Frequency: Daily   Weekly   Monthly   Other:_____

Duration: _____

Location: _____

Goal #5: _____

_____

_____

Frequency: Daily   Weekly   Monthly   Other:_____

Duration: _____

Location: _____

Goal #6: _____

_____

_____

Frequency: Daily   Weekly   Monthly   Other:_____

Duration: _____

Location: _____

3. EMOTIONAL HEALTH/MANAGING WORRY

Goal #1: _____

_____

_____

Frequency: Daily   Weekly   Monthly   Other: _____

Duration: _____

Location: _____

Goal #2: _____

_____

_____

Frequency: Daily   Weekly   Monthly   Other: _____

Duration: _____

Location: _____

Goal #3: _____

_____

_____

Frequency: Daily   Weekly   Monthly   Other: _____

Duration: _____

Location: _____

Goal #4: _____

_____

_____

Frequency: Daily   Weekly   Monthly   Other:_____

Duration: _____

Location: _____

Goal #5: _____

_____

_____

Frequency: Daily   Weekly   Monthly   Other:_____

Duration: _____

Location: _____

Goal #6: _____

_____

_____

Frequency: Daily   Weekly   Monthly   Other:_____

Duration: _____

Location: _____

4. RELATIONSHIP HEALTH

Goal #1: _____

_____

_____

Frequency: Daily   Weekly   Monthly   Other:_____

Duration: _____

Location: _____

Goal #2: _____

_____

_____

Frequency: Daily   Weekly   Monthly   Other:_____

Duration: _____

Location: _____

Goal #3: _____

_____

_____

Frequency: Daily   Weekly   Monthly   Other:_____

Duration: _____

Location: _____

Goal #4: _____

_____

_____

Frequency: Daily   Weekly   Monthly   Other:_____

Duration: _____

Location: _____

Goal #5: _____

_____

_____

Frequency: Daily   Weekly   Monthly   Other:_____

Duration: _____

Location: _____

Goal #6: _____

_____

_____

Frequency: Daily   Weekly   Monthly   Other:_____

Duration: _____

Location: _____

5. SPIRITUAL HEALTH

Goal #1: _____

_____

_____

Frequency: Daily   Weekly   Monthly   Other:_____

Duration: _____

Location: _____

Goal #2: _____

_____

_____

Frequency: Daily   Weekly   Monthly   Other:_____

Duration: _____

Location: _____

Goal #3: _____

_____

_____

Frequency: Daily   Weekly   Monthly   Other:_____

Duration: _____

Location: _____

Goal #4: _____

_____

_____

Frequency: Daily   Weekly   Monthly   Other:_____

Duration: _____

Location: _____

Goal #5: _____

_____

_____

Frequency: Daily   Weekly   Monthly   Other:_____

Duration: _____

Location: _____

Goal #6: _____

_____

_____

Frequency: Daily   Weekly   Monthly   Other:_____

Duration: _____

Location: _____

Conclusion

"Be who you are and be that well."

— Saint Francis de Sales

Acknowledging and embracing your self-worth is the key to being the most authentic version of yourself. When you make your well-being a priority, you send the message to yourself and others that you know your own value. Remember that when you are tired, stressed, overwhelmed, and don't like yourself very much, it's harder to be fully present to others, whether with your family, friends, or coworkers. But when you take care of your physical, mental, emotional, and spiritual well-being, you are able to be more fully present to the world and those around you.

At first, it might seem unnatural to prioritize yourself, to set boundaries, and to say no to the things you can't or don't want to do, but once you experience the benefits, you will see that it's absolutely worth the effort. Taking care of yourself is not an end in and of itself. Rather, it is a means to an end. Your goal is to embrace and believe in your self-worth as a child of God, so that you can live an authentic life in the unique way you are called to. You have a one-of-a-kind combination of gifts that no one else in the world has, and you have a purpose in life that no one else can fulfill. Taking care of yourself enables you to embrace that purpose freely and completely.

Embracing an attitude of self-love doesn't mean a drastic career change or a cross-country move. Instead, it means choosing little ways to take care of yourself every day. A Self-Care Action Plan will help guide you as you start the journey, and it will get easier and easier as you go along.

You've chosen to take an important and life-changing step toward becoming a better version of yourself. When you begin to believe that you are a gift and that you are worth taking care of, you can then embrace whatever you are called to in life, and you will be able to give yourself more generously, more honestly, and more joyfully to the people God has placed in your life.

Appendices

Sample Personalized Self-Care Action Plans

Case Example #1: Monica

Monica is a busy mom of three who struggles to make time for herself after a busy day of taking care of her family. She feels like each day is a blur, rushing from housework to errands, driving her kids around, and juggling a small side business from her home. She crashes each night for about five hours of sleep, only to get up and do it all over again. She is perpetually exhausted and struggles to make her own health a priority. She knows intellectually that it is important to press pause throughout her busy days, to make sure she has ten minutes here and there to eat, call a friend, or even spend time journaling or reading Scripture, but she usually finds it easier to justify ignoring her needs in favor of her family or her business.

She is overwhelmed by the thought of starting a self-care plan, but she's tired and knows change is needed. She has decided to give it a try, to see if she can experience the benefits of taking care of herself, not only for herself but also for her family. Monica wants to start simple, and she will add to her plan as she starts seeing results.

Monica's Self-Care Action Plan
(Pay attention to the SMART goal specifications)

PHYSICAL HEALTH
Goal #1: Get a minimum of seven hours of sleep a night

Frequency: Daily

Duration: Be in bed by 10:30 p.m. in order to be asleep by 11:00 and wake up at 6:00 a.m. (which will still give time to be up before the kids to make breakfast and help them get ready for the day)

Location: Bedroom. No TV or being on the phone after 9:00 p.m. Read a book or journal as part of bedtime routine.

Goal #2: Take twenty minutes around lunch to prepare and eat a simple but well-balanced meal

Frequency: Daily

Duration: Lunchtime

Location: At home. Keep fridge stocked with healthy meal options found online.

MENTAL HEALTH
Goal #2: Change self-critical statements into positive (or more realistic) statements about myself

Frequency: Daily

Duration: Ongoing

Location: Primarily when feeling stressed or rushed

EMOTIONAL HEALTH/MANAGING WORRY
Goal #1: Identify feelings when stressed and turn it into a problem-solving opportunity

Frequency: Ongoing

Duration: Less than five minutes

Location: Any location

RELATIONSHIP HEALTH

Goal #1: Call a friend at least once a week for a fifteen-minute conversation

Frequency: Weekly

Duration: Fifteen minutes

Location: At home or while taking a walk (to sneak in some exercise!)

SPIRITUAL HEALTH

Goal #1: Spend five minutes a day focused solely on prayer using a daily reflection (like Blessed is She website) as a prompt

Frequency: Daily

Duration: Five minutes

Location: At the kitchen table while the kids are at school

Goal #2: Subscribe to a spiritual podcast to listen to while doing housework and running errands

Frequency: Daily

Duration: Half-hour

Location: While doing housework or running errands

Case Example #2: Charlie

Charlie is a young professional who works for a law firm, which means he works long hours surrounded by paperwork and running from meetings with clients to court appearances. He loves his job but thinks that his boss doesn't acknowledge his full potential. Plus, with his busy schedule, he hasn't exercised regularly in the past six months, gets about five hours of sleep a night, relies on takeout for most of his meals, counts drinking on weekends as his only social activity, and finds himself worrying a lot about his workload and the fact that he hasn't dated anyone in several months.

Charlie's Self-Care Action Plan

(Pay attention to the SMART goal specifications)

PHYSICAL HEALTH

Goal #1: Get seven hours of sleep a night

Frequency: Daily

Duration: Be in bed by 10:00 p.m. in order to be asleep by 10:30 and wake up at 5:30 a.m., which will be seven hours of sleep.

Location: Bedroom. Prepare room for sleep by buying blackout curtains, turning off all lights, keeping the room cool, and using a white-noise machine

Goal #2: Opt for a salad with lean protein for at least one meal a day, even if it's takeout

Frequency: Daily

Duration: Lunchtime

Location: Office (when ordering in) and at restaurants when out for meetings

Goal #3: Exercise by taking a kickboxing class twice a week.

Frequency: Twice a week on Tuesdays and Thursdays

Duration: Fifty-minute class

Location: Kickboxing gym two blocks from office

MENTAL HEALTH

Goal #1: Make time twice a week to read (leisure activity)

Frequency: Twice a week, on Wednesdays in the evening and Sundays in the afternoon

Duration: Twenty to thirty minutes

Location: Home

Goal #2: Identify when my inner critic is talking and challenge those thoughts

Frequency: Daily

Duration: Ongoing

Location: Primarily at work

EMOTIONAL HEALTH/MANAGING WORRY

Goal #1: Manage worry by setting an alarm during the day to practice being present

Frequency: Daily

Duration: Five minutes a day, three times a day

Location: At the office and before going to bed

RELATIONSHIP HEALTH

Goal #1: Schedule activities with friends in the evenings and on weekends that don't necessarily involve drinking

Frequency: Weekly

Duration: One to two hours

Location: Various locations

Goal #2: Have conversation with boss about how to better manage workload and to better take on a greater leadership role

Frequency: One-time conversation with potential for follow-up

Duration: One hour (not including prep time)

Location: Lunch with boss

Goal #3: Ask friends to set me up with potential dates

Frequency: Monthly

Duration: Ongoing

Location: Ask friends by phone call or in person

SPIRITUAL HEALTH

Goal #1: Stop by the church to pray on the way to work twice a week

Frequency: Twice a week, on Tuesdays and Thursdays after kickboxing, but before work

Duration: Ten to fifteen minutes

Location: Church that is down the street from work

Goal #2: Subscribe to Bishop Robert Barron's Daily Gospel Reflection email

Frequency: Daily

Duration: Five to ten minutes

Location: At kitchen table over morning coffee

Suggested Reading

If you are interested in learning more about topics covered in this book, I've listed some helpful resources below. Many of these books are sitting on my own office bookshelf!

Boundaries
- *Boundaries* by Drs. Cloud and Townsend

Mindfulness
- *Mindfulness* by Mark Williams and Danny Penman
- *The Mindful Catholic: Finding God One Moment at a Time* by Gregory Battaro, PsyD (https://catholicmindfulness.teachable.com/p/catholic-mindfulness)

Mental Health
- *Catholic Guide to Depression* by Dr. Aaron Kheriaty
- *The Depression Workbook* by Mary Ellen Copeland, MS, MA
- *The Anxiety & Phobia Workbook* by Edmund J. Bourne, PhD

Relationships
- *The Seven Principles for Making Marriage Work* by John Gottman, PhD
- *The Five Love Languages* by Gary Chapman

Self-Improvement
- *The Happiness Project* by Gretchen Rubin
- *Better Than Before* by Gretchen Rubin
- *The Four Tendencies* by Gretchen Rubin

Self-Worth
- *The Gifts of Imperfection* by Brene Brown
- *Man's Search for Meaning* by Viktor Frankl
- *Born Only Once* by Conrad Baars, MD

Spirituality
- *Discernment of Spirits: An Ignatian Guide for Everyday Living* by Timothy M. Gallagher, OMV
- *The Second Greatest Story Ever Told* by Fr. Michael Gaitley
- *Introduction to the Devout Life* by Saint Francis de Sales

Acknowledgments

"No man is an island," John Donne wrote, and the same sentiment could be said about this book, because it most certainly wasn't written in a vacuum.

I am indebted to my family and friends who willingly lent their ears when I needed to talk through an idea (again and again and again), offered a refreshingly new perspective when I felt stuck, and showered me with words of support and encouragement throughout the entire process.

I am grateful for my professors, mentors, priests and other religious, and fellow professionals who helped shape my worldview and encouraged me to have the confidence to use my voice for good.

I am deeply thankful for all of my clients who have taught me so much about the power of courage and resilience in the face of adversity. I have been privileged to witness how transformative embracing your self-worth can truly be.

Mary Beth, my editor, the designers, marketers, editors, and the entire Our Sunday Visitor team have made the whole book-writing process as easy as writing a book can possibly be. Mary Beth's gentle guidance and expertise have been an incredible gift during this amazing experience.

Each and every one of you have helped to make this book much better than I ever could do on my own. Thank you!

Notes

1. "Get Enough Sleep," U.S. Department of Health and Human Services, accessed February 12, 2018, https://healthfinder.gov/ HealthTopics/Category/everyday-healthy-living/ mental-health-and-relationship/get-enough-sleep#the-basics_2.

2. "Consequences of Insufficient Sleep," Division of Sleep Medicine, Harvard Medical School, accessed February 12, 2018, http://healthysleep .med.harvard.edu/healthy/matters/consequences.

3. U.S. Department of Health and Human Services and National Heart, Lung, and Blood Institute, *Your Guide to Healthy Sleep* (NIH Publication No. 11-5271, November 2005, revised August 2011), https://www.nhlbi.nih .gov/files/docs/public/sleep/healthy_sleep.pdf.

4. Eva Selhub, MD, "Nutritional psychiatry: Your brain on food," Harvard Health Publishing, Harvard Medical School, November 16, 2015, https://www.health.harvard.edu/blog/ nutritional-psychiatry-your-brain-on-food-201511168626.

5. Ibid.

6. Kirsten Wier, "The exercise effect," American Psychological Association *Monitor on Psychology*, December 2011, Vol. 42, No. 11, http:// www.apa.org/monitor/2011/12/exercise.aspx/.

7. Ibid.

8. Ashish Sharma, MD, Vishal Madaan, MD, and Frederick D. Petty, MD, PhD, "Exercise for Mental Health," *Prim Care Companion J Clin Psychiatry*, 2006 8(2): 106, https://www.ncbi.nlm.nih.gov/pmc/articles/ PMC1470658/.

9. "How much physical activity do adults need?" Centers for Disease Control and Prevention, accessed February 12, 2018, https://www.cdc.gov/physicalactivity/basics/adults/index.htm.

10. Daphne M. Davis, Ph.D., and Jeffrey A. Hayes, Ph.D., "What are the benefits of mindfulness" American Psychological Association, *Monitor on Psychology*, July/August 2012, http://www.apa.org/monitor/2012/07-08/ce-corner.aspx.

11. Christina N. Armenta and Sonja Lyubomirsky, "How Gratitude Motivates Us to Become Better People," UC Berkeley's *Greater Good Magazine*, May 23, 2017, https://greatergood.berkeley.edu/article/item/how_gratitude_motivates_us_to_become_better_people.

12. Joel Wong and Joshua Brown, "How Gratitude Changes You and Your Brain," UC Berkeley, *Greater Good Magazine*, June 6, 2017, https://greatergood.berkeley.edu/article/item/how_gratitude_changes_you_and_your_brain.

13. "Writing about emotions may ease stress and trauma," Harvard Health Publishing, https://www.health.harvard.edu/healthbeat/writing-about-emotions-may-ease-stress-and-trauma.

14. "Spirituality," University of Maryland Medical Center, accessed February 12, 2018, http://www.umm.edu/health/medical/altmed/treatment/spirituality.

15. Beth Azar, "A reason to believe," American Psychological Association, *Monitor on Psychology*, December 2010, Vol. 41, No. 11, http://www.apa.org/monitor/2010/12/believe.aspx.

16. Piercarlo Valdesolo, "Scientists Find One Source of Prayer's Power," *Scientific American*, December 24, 2013, https://www.scientificamerican.com/article/scientists-find-one-source-of-prayers-power/.

17. "Achieving your goals: An evidence-based approach," Michigan State University Extension, August 26, 2014, http://msue.anr.msu.edu/news/achieving_your_goals_an_evidence_based_approach.